British Rail
Operations
in the 1980s

Plate 1:   A typical scene from the British Rail network of the 1980s is the High Speed Train or IC125. From the introduction of the first set, on the Western Region in 1976, for use on the Paddington—Bristol and South Wales routes, to the autumn of 1982 when the final set was commissioned, 198 power cars and 702 trailer vehicles were constructed. In this illustration, Western Region-allocated set No. 253030 passes through the Cornish countryside, near Cutmere, with the 07.25 Paddington—Penzance service on 20th June 1980.

Colin Marsden

BRITISH RAIL OPERATIONS IN THE 1980s

Colin Marsden

Plate 2: Throughout the late 1970s and early 1980s, many enthusiasts have given their attention to the BREL Works at Doncaster where the Class 56 locomotives have been in production. Standing outside the paint shop, in immaculate condition, prior to operating the works test train to Scunthorpe, on 12th September 1981, is No. 56097.

Colin Marsden

Oxford Publishing Company

Typesetting by:
Aquarius Typesetting Services, New Milton, Hants.

Printed in Great Britain by:
Netherwood Dalton & Co. Ltd., Huddersfield,
Yorks.

Published by:
Oxford Publishing Co.
Link House
West Street
POOLE, Dorset

Plate 3:   One of the Southern's most modern electric multiple unit trains, of Class 508, slowly departs from Clapham
Junction, on a snowy 15th December 1981, and is bound for Hampton Court. When delivered to the Southern Region,
late in 1979, these 43 units, forming the Class 508 derivative of the 1972 design high density stock, were the first new
units built for the region since 1974.

Colin Marsden

INTRODUCTION

Today, with many more railway enthusiasts than ever before, the interest in selected spheres of railway operation is becoming quite common. This is particularly noticeable where locomotives of a particular type are involved.

This book has been prepared to give readers an insight into some of the more important rail operations in the 1980s. Each section has an introduction which is followed by a selection of illustrations of the specific operation.

From the birth of the railways, operations have gradually become more sophisticated, with complex computer-based diagramming of locomotives and stock, complicated freight diagramming, advanced locomotive building, the quest for higher speed and the rebuilding of some locomotives for use into the 21st century.

It is hoped that readers will find this book of assistance in understanding specific railway operations and their purpose.

I should like to record my thanks to many colleagues of BR, Mr B. Ault and Mr D. Porter of BREL, Freightliners Ltd., and the many photographic contributors who have assisted with material for this volume.

Colin J. Marsden
Surbiton
September 1983

CLASS 50 REFURBISHING

Following the transfer of Class 50 locomotives to the Western Region from the Midland Region, between 1973 and 1976, the service availability of the class dropped from 67 per cent, whilst working on the Midland, to a wholly unacceptable 39 per cent in their first full year on the Western Region, thereby rendering it almost impossible, on occasions, for the region to give a full main line passenger service. The maintenance of the locomotives, while operating on the Midland and Scottish regions, was almost entirely carried out by Crewe and Carlisle depots who, from the introduction of this class, had been associated with their upkeep and had come to terms with the many problems that were not part of the laid down maintenance procedure. Once on the Western Region the allocation was divided between Old Oak Common (London), Bristol Bath Road and Plymouth (Laira). All had vast experience of diesel-hydraulic locomotives, but little experience on the diesel-electric transmission principle, with the exception of inter-regional locomotives. The classified works' overhaul of the class was undertaken, from their introduction, by Crewe Works until January 1977, when it was decided to concentrate the majority of English Electric locomotive repairs at the Doncaster Workshops. With the unacceptable availability rate for the locomotives during 1977/78, only one remedy was on the cards; that of the major rebuilding of a comparatively modern 10 year old locomotive.

The CM&EE section at Derby drew up plans for a complete rebuild from the shell upwards, and the removal of sophisticated electronic systems previously carried and other redundant equipment. When built, in 1967/68, by the English Electric Company at Vulcan Foundry, the D400 class were the first main line diesel-electric locomotives to be fitted with solid state electronic equipment for the control of the main generator output, electronic wheel-slip protection systems and driver pre-set tractive effort equipment. Also fitted, for the first time on a main line diesel locomotive, was dynamic braking, using the 'back' power from the traction motors to retard road speed, which was, of course, in addition to standard air and vacuum brake equipment.

One of the BR directives, at the construction of this class, was the fitting of inertia air filtration equipment, which comprised primary and secondary disposable dry pack elements, fitted in place of the time-honoured oil-wetted type. The air system provided 'clean' air for the traction motors, turbo blowers and the dynamic brake equipment compartment, all dirt being removed from the air by a motor driven fan. Another fitting applied to these locomoties which, over the years, has proved of little use, was the slow-speed traction control unit. This enabled the driver to pre-select a required low range speed and, via electronic equipment, the speed of the locomotive would remain constant at between ½ and 5 mph.

After protracted discussions between the Western Region CM&EE and the Chief CM&EE Department of the BRB, together with BREL, it was decided that a full refurbishing scheme for the class, with a view to prolonging the lives of the locomotives for up to 20 years, or at least into the 21st century, was desirable. As Doncaster Works had taken over responsibility for the class from 1977, it was decided that they would undertake the mammoth rebuilding programme, and by late 1978 all was ready for the acceptance of the first locomotive. However No. 50006 *Neptune*, which arrived at the works on 29th September 1977 with various defects and was still on works at the end of 1978 without any work having been done on it, was a prime candidate for the prototype refurbished locomotive and was officially reclassified as undergoing general/refurbish repairs on 2nd January 1979.

As many of the problems had been attributable to dirt content in the internal air of the locomotives, a completely new air system was to be installed. Initially the air was drawn in through the inertia filtration equipment, near the main and auxiliary generators but, unfortunately, in addition to the air passing through the filters, dirt, oil and brake dust penetrated the body louvres and filters, and contaminated the 'clean air' compartments which caused the general interior to become very dirty. On several occasions this was confirmed as being the cause of generator armature flashovers. To alleviate this problem the refurbishing programme called for a new bulkhead to be constructed which separated the electrical equipment (main and auxiliary generators) from the engine compartment, and the installation of new Vokes filtration equipment. A fan was also installed in the roof, together with additional side grilles in one of the former engine-room windows. A further operational problem, which in later years was isolated, was caused by the dynamic or rheostatic brake equipment. When fitted, during the 1960s, the equipment was considered somewhat revolutionary but, in practice the system proved totally unsatisfactory on diesel locomotives. During refurbishment, this equipment was completely removed and the space utilized to accommodate some of the new air filtration equipment. Whilst the locomotives were stripped down, a complete rewire, using the latest heat resistant and fire insulated cable, was carried out.

When the Class 50s were introduced, during 1967/68, many people were surprised to see a slow speed control (SSC) system installed, this fitted with the intention that the locomotives may, one day, be utilized on merry-go-round coal trains when their useful life was finished on the West Coast Main Line passenger services. But, alas, this was not to be and, during the refurbishing programme, this equipment was removed completely. Another feature built into the locomotives was a wheel-slip sanding system. This, again, was isolated for many years and finally removed, and the resulting holes on the body side were plated over. In both cabs and engine room, as well as underfloor, much of the original English Electric Company piping and cabling has been replaced and repositioned, thus enabling further works examinations to be easier. The driving cabs which, when built, contained SSC and tractive effort pre-set equipment, have been completely re-designed but the actual power and brake controllers are still of the same design. Apart from replacing a bodyside window as a ventilator, and the plating over of the distinctive roof recess at No. 2 end, the body design has not been altered, except for the fitting of a centrally-situated high-powered headlight in the nose end. This headlight is now a standard requirement for new and refurbished main line diesel and electric locomotives. At an early stage in the refurbishing programme, it was rumoured that the now redundant roof-mounted headcode boxes would be removed in favour of two white marker lights on the locomotive front, but this modification was not carried out.

The first two locomotives to receive general/refurbish repairs, Nos. 50006 *Neptune* and 50003 *Temeraire*, were not actually called to works for this repair and arrived for normal general overhaul, but were reclassified as refurbished whilst on works. The input of locomotives should be on a maintenance cycle, but due to failures or collisions in traffic, several substitutions have been made. When a locomotive is called to works for general/refurbish repairs, it is operated to Doncaster by the first suitable service. If suffering a failure or collision damage, a special pathway is arranged, or the locomotive may be formed into a freight train, and conveyed as a fitted vehicle, for its journey north. After arrival on works it is placed on the 'plant line' where initial inspection of the required repairs takes place, and the batteries and some equipment are usually removed at this stage. The locomotive is then de-fuelled and taken to the stripping shop at the far end of the works. Here all components, including bogies, are removed, cleaned and sent to the respective shops around the works.

A Class 50 locomotive normally spends some 4 to 5 days under stripping and internal cleaning prior to being mounted on trolley bogies and being hauled to the paint shop where a full internal repaint, in grey, takes place. On some of the later refurbished locomotives, the complete external body paintwork was removed with paint stripper and repainted in green primer. From the paint shop, and still mounted on trolley bogies, the shell is taken to the main works and admitted to No. 4 bay where the shell is placed on stands. The first job undertaken is the replacing of any defective bodywork panels or the repairs to any collision-damaged areas. The plating over of the lower roof section and the fitting of the new compartment side grille, as well as the cutting of the headlamp orifice, now takes

place. Following body repairs and alterations the actual reassembly work begins. Firstly the electric unit frame is installed, this having been assembled in another part of the works. For the next 2 to 3 weeks the locomotive is in the hands of the electricians who install and wire up the various pieces of new equipment. Following this, the brake frame and associated equipment is refitted, and this is then fully tested. The new Vokes air filtration equipment comes next followed by other large items such as air compressors, vacuum exhauster, radiator equipment, to name but a few. Finally, the main power unit and generators are replaced. All equipment will have been repaired in various parts of the works and this means that it will not necessarily be returned to the locomotive from which it was removed!

Now the main items have been reinstalled, smaller parts, including the driving cab modules, are now refitted and the final wiring is carried out. While the actual locomotive is under repair in the works No. 4 bay, the bogies are maintained in the bogie shop adjoining the locomotive shop. Again, it is unlikely that the same pair of bogies will be replaced on the same engine as that on which they arrived. After about 10 to 12 weeks in the main shop, the locomotive is married up with bogies and taken outside where, after initial inspection, it is fuelled, watered, lubricated and started up by the works test engineers for the first time. After initial testing, and the setting up of various tolerances, the locomotive is placed in the test house for a stringent test programme involving the running of the power unit under various load conditions, after which it proceeds to the paint shop.

The first six refurbished locomotives were outshopped in standard livery, but following repairs to No. 50023 *Howe* a new revised livery was applied. In the paint shop the first job is to remove old paint and, depending on the condition of the body, filler is applied. Sometimes the whole body is smoothed over, but more often than not only particular areas are dealt with. After a rub down the body is ready for painting. The blue is applied first followed by the yellow ends, the grey roof and, finally, the black cab windows and underframe. The last job is to apply the large logo and running number, which are all hand-painted, to tidy up the nameplate and apply front end and underframe detail. After release from the paint shop a thorough inspection, by the works CM&EE Department, takes place prior to a road test being arranged.

As with any item of equipment that has been completely stripped down and rebuilt, the testing is of prime importance. Although most faults are normally found whilst the 'on works' testing takes place, it is essential, for a reasonably long distance trial, utilizing the locomotive at its full output, to be carried out. For this, a works test train, formed of former coaching stock vehicles, is used between Doncaster and York or Newcastle. Up to the end of 1981 the works test train consisted of a rake of former LMS 'B' vans, being fitted with vacuum brake only and not having electric train heating equipment. However a new dual-braked, dual-heated test train came into operation late in 1981 and was more suitable for the Class 50s. If any further faults are found, after a trial run, the locomotive returns to works for rectification. This is very unusual as the level of workmanship is of a very high standard. However, it is recorded that No. 50035 *Ark Royal* operated no less than 8 test trains and 9 test trains were ascribed to No.

50025 *Invincible*. Once a satisfactory test run is achieved and final inspection has been carried out, the locomotive is handed back to the running department and placed in the transfer siding ready for collection by the traffic department. Locomotives usually run to the nearby diesel depot from where a return service to the Western Region is found.

Up to the end of 1981 locomotives usually returned to the Western Region at the head of the Edinburgh—Plymouth service, and were attached at either York or Sheffield. However, after the change of this train to IC125 operation, locomotives usually operate light engine to Sheffield and work services to Bristol or Birmingham and thence to the Western Region. After arriving back on Western Region metals, it is usual for locomotives to operate to their home depot for examination, prior to re-entering revenue-earning traffic, and hopefully not having to return to Doncaster Works again for at least four years.

Plate 4 (above): After the demise of the Class 52 'Western' locomotives, in 1976, many enthusiasts turned their attention to other forms of traction, and a considerable number pledged their allegiance to the Class 50 locomotives built by the English Electric Company. At the time of their introduction on the Western Region, during the mid-1970s, it was not envisaged that in years to come the whole class would be refurbished. Two such examples, Nos. 50022 *Anson* and 50035 *Ark Royal*, are illustrated here standing outside the maintenance shed at Old Oak Common.

Colin Marsden

Plate 5 (below): Apart from livery variations on refurbished locomotives, the easiest way of identifying a refurbished example is by the headlamp, which is applied midway up the body on the nose end section. Here No. 50036 *Victorious*, looking rather tatty, pulls out of Parsons Tunnel, near Dawlish, with the 08.15 Birmingham—Plymouth train on 30th September 1980.

Colin Marsden

Plate 6 (above): Prior to the refurbishing scheme being authorized, availability of the Class 50 locomotives for general traffic was decreasing, and on some occasions an availability rate of under 50 per cent was recorded. Locomotive No. 50042 *Triumph* did not arrive at the works for refurbishing until 6th January 1982, but when photographed on 24th May 1980 the body was starting to show signs of decay and was in need of attention. Here No. 50042 is pictured hauling a Paddington—Bristol express out of Box Tunnel.

Colin Marsden

Plate 7 (left): The selection of locomotives to visit works is not always taken on a strict maintenance rotation and is dependent on any major break-down of serviceable locomotives. Two Class 20 locomotives, Nos. 20186 and 20176 are seen here, hauling Class 50, No. 50037 *Illustrious* towards the Lickey Incline, on 27th October 1981 while en route from the Western Region to Doncaster Works for routine maintenance. The Class 50 was being towed due to some of its technical components having already been removed.

Mark Swift

Plate 8 (above): After locomotives are accepted on works for repair, the first job is to de-fuel them to ensure complete safety throughout all operations, as much of the work will involve the use of cutting and heat equipment. After being de-fuelled, the loco-motive is taken to the stripping shop where all items are removed and sent to the respective shops in the works for repair. Parked outside the stripping shop, on 9th January 1981, stands No. 50010 *Monarch.*

Colin Marsden

Plate 9 (below): Looking rather more messy than usual, following a serious fire in the roof of the building, Class 50 No. 50039 *Implacable* stands in the works stripping shop. Here all internal equipment is removed, prior to the locomotive being taken to the paint shop for pre-assembly painting. By the nature of the work undertaken in this shop, it is one of the least clean in the works.

Plate 10 (left): To enable locomotives to be transported around the works, once they have visited the stripping shop and have had their bogies removed, trolley bogies are provided, as illustrated here on No. 50016 *Barham*. The locomotive was photographed, on 21st August 1982, en route from the stripping shop to the paint shop for internal painting.

J. Patel

Plate 12 (right): Throughout the Class 50 refurbishing programme, the works No. 4 bay has always been used for the repairs and re-assembly operations, with usually up to five locomotives, in various stages of repair, being dealt with at one time. In this view, taken during May 1982, No. 50005 *Collingwood* and No. 50048 *Dauntless* are seen receiving first stage re-assembly.

J. Patel

Plate 11 (below): Mounted on former Class 24 trolley bogies, Class 50 No. 50013 *Agincourt* stands in the paint shop whilst the internal painting is carried out. It is far easier to clean the interior of the locomotive when all equipment has been removed, rather than doing the best possible after the new equipment is in situ. It will be noticed that some of the draw gear items have been removed.

Colin Marsden

Plate 13 (right): Depending on the condition of components, some locomotives have their multiple control jumper equipment removed while in the stripping shop, but the two illustrated here still retain this fitment. No. 50012 *Benbow* can be seen soon after arriving from pre-painting and prior to the headlamp orifice being cut and sand-box ports being plated over.

Colin Marsden

Plate 14 (above): Much of the external body filling and side alterations had already taken place when this view of No. 50036 *Victorious* was taken on 22nd April 1981. The two sand-box filler points have been plated over and the small oblong window in the engine compartment has been replaced by a ventilator. The bank of missing radiator grilles will be replaced at a later date and this space serves as access for various items of internal equipment.

J. Pate.

Plate 15 (left): Involved in the general/refurbishing repair is a complete rewire, a mammoth job that can take skilled electricians up to 21 days to complete. Here No. 50020 *Revenge* stands in the works No. 4 bay during the early stages of rewiring. Cables can be seen protruding from the marker light sockets and leading to the train heating jumper receptacle.

Colin Marsden

Plate 16 (right): If a locomotive arrives with collision damage, the repairs are carried out as soon as the locomotive enters the main erecting shop and prior to any re-assembly work taking place. No. 50038 *Formidable*, having suffered considerable side damage, shows the mass of new panelling fitted. It is interesting to note that, although considerable work has been undertaken, the nameplate remains in place.

Colin Marsden

Plate 17 (below): On 5th March 1982, No. 50048 *Dauntless* was admitted to the works, but apart from inspection, work did not commence until 23rd March. After spending two weeks in the stripping shop and receiving pre-painting to the internal framing, the locomotive took its place in No. 4 bay where it remained for the next three months. When photographed, on 16th May 1982, the body was awaiting re-assembly. It is interesting to note that locomotives dealt with during 1982 have had their front ends painted in primer soon after arrival at the works.

J. Patel

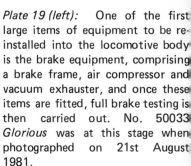

Plate 18 (left): While undergoing repairs inside the workshops each locomotive is mounted on trestles, or jacks, these being a little taller than the normal locomotive height. Locomotives are placed on these stands, rather than on bogies, to enable the engineers to have free access to underframe equipment. No. 50045 *Achilles*, illustrated here during April 1981, shows that all front end items, including the buffer beam and former headcode box equipment, have been removed.

J. Patel

Plate 20 (right): The actual locomotive body under repair waits in No. 4 bay for the refitment of its major components. These have been overhauled in various buildings throughout the works and, due to the time delay for subsidiary repairs, much of the equipment may not necessarily be returned to the same locomotive from which it was removed. Looking rather worse for wear, No. 50031 *Hood* awaits re-assembly during August 1981.

J. Patel

Plate 19 (left): One of the first large items of equipment to be re-installed into the locomotive body is the brake equipment, comprising a brake frame, air compressor and vacuum exhauster, and once these items are fitted, full brake testing is then carried out. No. 50033 *Glorious* was at this stage when photographed on 21st August 1981.

J. Patel

Plate 21 (right): In addition to the refurbishment programme, various Class 31, 37 and 56 locomotives had to be fitted in for their regular maintenance and, therefore, a stringent shopping programme had always to be adhered to, thus ensuring that sufficient space was available in the shops when required. No. 50008 *Thunderer* awaits engine replacement during September 1981.

J. Patel

Plate 22 (left): After re-assembly of all items, the locomotive is married up with a pair of bogies that will have received attention in the bogie shop, and when all the running requirements such as oil, water and diesel fuel have been supplied, testing can begin. During testing each locomotive visits the weighshop for weighing and it is outside this shop that No. 50045 *Achilles* stands during late July 1981. Much of the body has been pre-filled at this stage and the locomotive is waiting for its turn in the paint shop.

Derek Porter

Plate 23 (below): The extent of external preparation required prior to painting, depends on the condition of the body. However all the general/refurbish locomotives receive a complete repaint. No. 50012 *Benbow*, shown here, has its front end daubed with undercoat on an otherwise filler-covered end. The bodyside has large areas of rubbed down filler visible.

Colin Marsden

Plate 24 (right): It is usual that locomotives which are required to be moved while in the paint shop, do not do so under their own power but are aided by one of the works pilot locomotives. Here, looking more like a ghost, No. 50040 *Leviathan* is positioned outside the paint shop while a Class 56 locomotive is removed from behind. The Class 50, at this stage, is covered in white/grey filler primer, which is applied prior to the top coat of paint.

Derek Porter

Plate 25 (below): Once a locomotive has been completed in the main works, it is unusual for it to return unless a failure occurs during testing or trial running. This was the case with No. 50008 *Thunderer* which suffered a minor failure during testing and was returned to No. 4 bay for rectification. As can be seen from this illustration, the standard of workmanship, applied to the bodywork, is of the highest, but after only a short time back in traffic the weather beaten effect will return.

Colin Marsden

Plate 26 (above): It is usual, unless a major failure occurs, for a locomotive to be between 3 and 4 weeks undergoing tests, painting and trial running, the time taken being dependent upon other works activities and the availability of the works test train for final trials. No. 50032 *Courageous*, resplendent in ex-works condition, runs through the works yard towards the buffer stops after completion, and before being returned to the Western Region.

Colin Marsden

Plate 27 (below): When the first six locomotives returned to traffic, they carried the conventional livery of rail blue body with full yellow warning ends, and the only way of recognizing these from a non-refurbished example was by the headlight fitting. No. 50019 *Ramillies* stands outside the main works buildings, awaiting return to the Western Region, on 28th March 1980. No. 50019 was only the fourth locomotive to receive a general/refurbish repair.

Colin Marsden

Locomotive number	Date on Works	Date work commenced	Date returned to traffic	Notes
50006	29.9.77	21.2.78	13.11.79	Originally called to works for general, and reclassified to general/refurbish on 2.1.79
50003	21.2.79	21.3.79	17.9.80	On works for collision repairs, reclassified to general/refurbish on 1.2.80
50017	21.6.79	26.7.79	5.2.80	
50019	27.7.79	14.9.79	31.3.80	Called as general and reclassified to general/refurbish on 1.10.79
50001	29.11.79	30.11.79	9.4.80	
50047	13.12.79	16.12.79	12.5.80	
50020	Called as general/refurbish repair, but cancelled due to No. 50013 requiring urgent attention			
50013	7.1.80	21.1.80	7.6.80	
50023	9.4.80	11.4.80	10.8.80	
50038	25.4.80	2.6.80	12.11.80	Repairs to collision damage
50004	2.5.80	8.5.80	29.10.80	
50022	28.5.80	11.6.80	19.12.80	
50032	15.8.80	18.8.80	31.11.80	
50015	11.9.80	17.9.80	11.2.81	
50020	14.10.80	15.10.80	6.3.81	
50035	5.11.80	20.11.80	27.3.81	Several failures on test prior to return to traffic
50012	5.11.80	20.11.80	5.5.81	Power unit change before return to traffic
50045	Called as general/refurbish repair, but cancelled due to No. 50010 requiring urgent attention			
50010	7.1.81	8.1.81	22.5.81	
50036	2.2.81	9.2.81	18.6.81	
50040	24.2.81	25.2.81	18.7.81	
50045	19.3.81	20.3.81	24.8.81	Prior to returning to traffic, it operated to Wolverton Works for Open Day on 22.8.81
50039	15.4.81	15.4.81	14.9.81	
50033	29.4.81	11.5.81	12.10.81	
50041	29.5.81	1.6.81	29.10.81	
50031	4.6.81	11.6.81	13.11.81	
50008	6.7.81	10.7.81	21.12.81	
50016	10.8.81	14.8.81	16.1.82	
50009	12.9.81	15.9.81	1.2.82	4 weeks late in returning to traffic due to power faults
50037	30.10.81	4.11.81	6.4.82	
50021	9.11.81	13.11.81	5.4.82	
50044	19.11.81	25.11.81	29.4.82	
50042	6.1.82	11.1.82	22.5.82	
50029	11.1.82	14.1.82	4.6.82	
50025	3.2.82	8.2.82	2.8.82	Delayed due to problems on test
50005	2.3.82	4.3.82	13.8.82	
50048	5.3.82	23.3.82	2.9.82	
50028	29.3.82	2.4.82	20.10.82	Suffered collision damage after completion
50034	27.5.82	31.5.82	25.10.82	
50024	8.6.82	10.6.82	15.11.82	
50007	Called as general/refurbish repair, but cancelled due to No. 50026 requiring urgent attention			
50026	27.7.82	2.8.82	6.12.82	
50018	6.8.82	12.8.82	20.12.82	
50007	13.9.82	16.9.82	28.2.83	
50046	11.10.82	4.11.82	19.3.83	
50011	22.11.82	26.11.82	15.4.83	
50043	6.12.82	8.12.82	4.5.83	
50049	11.1.83	17.1.83	28.5.83	
50050	17.1.83	26.1.83	5.7.83	
50027	7.2.83	2.3.83	23.7.83	
50030	31.3.83	11.4.83		
50002	31.3.83	25.4.83		
50014	23.5.83	26.5.83		

Plate 28: Although not a recognized fuelling point for 'in traffic' locomotives, the works has its own fuelling facilities which are positioned outside the weighshop. No. 50033 *Glorious* is pictured standing by the fuelling equipment, after loading, but prior to working the test train to Newcastle on 15th October 1981.

Colin Marsden

Plate 29 (left): One of the major attractions for rail enthusiasts in the north-east area is the testing of Class 50 locomotives, which is usually carried out between Doncaster and Newcastle. Up to the end of 1981, a train was formed of 7 or 8 former LMS-designed 'B' vans, which had been taken into departmental stock and used exclusively on the works test trains. In this view, No. 50040 *Leviathan* passes through Doncaster Station with a return test train on 19th June 1981.

Derek Porter

Plate 30 (right): The use of the standard 7–8 vehicle test train for trials on other works rebuilds was quite sufficient, but with the higher power output of the Class 50s a train of only 8 vehicles was too light, and the locomotive was operating below full power for a considerable portion of the trials. Many test engineers at Doncaster considered a train of 10 standard Mk I vehicles more suitable and, during 1982, a train fulfilling these requirements was supplied. In this view, taken from Hexthorpe Bridge, No. 50041 *Bulwark* departs with a northbound test train formed of one new Mk I and eight old LMS vehicles.

Derek Porter

Plate 31 (left): The return of locomotives from Doncaster to the Western Region has always been an operating nightmare. However, during 1981, it became regular operating practice for completed locomotives to run light engine to York and then work the Edinburgh–Plymouth service forward, but as this working was transferred to IC125 sets from early 1982, other trains have had to be found. When No. 50045 *Achilles* was completed, it went light engine to Wolverton Works for display at their Open Day. It is seen here, departing from Doncaster Works, on 21st August 1981.

Colin Marsden

Plate 32 (above): The first locomotive to be painted in the revised livery, No. 50023 *Howe*, was completed at Doncaster on 30th August 1980. It returned to the Western Region on 3rd September in charge of the 09.50 Edinburgh—Plymouth train and is pictured here arriving at Derby, where it gave many enthusiasts their first opportunity to see the revised livery.

Barry Nicolle

Plate 33 (below): Detail showing modified air intakes on refurbished locomotives. If this view is compared with an un-refurbished locomotive it will be observed that the recess in the roof has been plated over but, for some reason, on No. 50017 *Royal Oak* the front sand-box has not been plated over, as is required under the general/refurbish programme.

Colin Marsden

Plate 34 (left): Still painted in conven tional livery, but sporting the tell-tale refurbished headlamp, Class 50, No 50019 Ramillies approaches Truro with vans from Penzance to Plymouth on 26th June 1980. When back on the Western Region the refurbished examples pro vided a much better availability level which, at one time, was practically on par with Class 47 locomotives.

Colin Marsden

Plate 36 (right): Since their refurbishing much of the heavy freight workings, that operate on the south-western section of the Western Region, have been placed in the hands of Class 50 locomotives. One such train that regularly produces refurbished examples, during the summer of 1981, was the evening Plymouth Friary—Exeter Riverside mixed freight service. In this view, on 22nd June 1981, locomotive No. 50038 Formidable is providing the power for the train which is approaching Dawlish Warren.

Colin Marsden

Plate 35 (left): One of the early strong holds for the refurbished examples was the Waterloo—Exeter route, which, when the Class 50s took over from Class 33s at the end of 1979, suffered the worst availability record of any locomotives. To help alleviate this problem the Western Region endeavoured to use as many re furbished examples on this route as was operationally possible. Here, No. 50019 Ramillies approaches Clapham Junction on 2nd June 1981.

Colin Marsden

Plate 37 (right): Although the new livery looks very pleasing to the eye, it is not an easy job to keep it clean and res pectable. One problem with some of the earlier examples was the gradual dis appearance of grey paint from the route indicator box. Looking rather dirty under the station lighting at Waterloo, on 29th December 1980, No. 50023 Howe waits to depart with the 19.10 service for Exeter.

Colin Marsden

AIR-BRAKED BLOCK TRAFFIC

Right from the start of railways, in the early 1800s, one of the largest uses of the system has been for freight transportation. Originally goods and materials were transported in open or covered un-braked trucks, a method which continued for some 100 years.

During the middle of the present century, various 'fitted' wagon stock emerged, 'fitted' being railway slang for a vehicle supplied with a continuous brake, a brake that is capable of being applied by four means: (1) by the driver, (2) by the guard (3) by accidental division of the train or derailment and (4) by a passenger communication valve, (PCV) in the case of passenger carrying vehicles. The basic method of supplying this continuous brake to goods vehicles, was to fit a vacuum cylinder and brake rigging, which was connected throughout the braked portion of the train, to the locomotive via end hoses, the vacuum being created by one or more air exhausters fitted on the locomotive. Vacuum is measured in inches and in normal railway circles the maximum required is 21 in., but on certain former GWR vehicles the requirement was 25 in. which caused some difficulty if the two types came together. The vacuum brake system, although very basic, is highly reliable and is still in operation on both passenger and freight stock throughout the BR system, and is likely to be in use for many years to come.

The operation under review in this section is air-braked block traffic; a comparatively new railway operation. Many large firms such as oil and cement companies have, for many years, used rail transportation for over 60 per cent of their total output, and during the late 1960s and early 1970s the British Railways Board and private wagon companies offered attractive terms, to selected companies, to hire or purchase complete trains. The railways soon saw large numbers of stone, powdered chemicals, aggregate and coal trains, formed completely of private owner or leasing company wagon stock, using their tracks. One of the largest owner/leasing companies is Procor Limited, of Horbury, near Wakefield, and many of the block trains now in service carry the insignia of this company. The company-owned freight trains are normally formed into non-permanently coupled sets, known as block loads, with the total number of wagons in any one set being dependent on the weight/quantity and type of commodity being transported.

British Rail also operate a sizeable fleet of their own air brake-fitted freight vehicles, and a considerable number of these operate on the 'Railfreight' and 'Speedlink' services, where the smaller customer can hire one or more vehicles of a booked freight train, an operation which is currently growing following the slight upward trend of taking goods off the roads and placing them back on the railways.

Plate 39 (above): Although this section deals with air brake-fitted trains, a few of the older style vacuum brake-fitted examples are illustrated. The train shown here, could well be confused with an air-braked block train, but it is, in fact, a formation of Blue Circle cement wagons, fitted only with the continuous vacuum brake. In this illustration the train is passing Brightside, on 10th September 1981, headed by Class 40 No. 40197.

Colin Marsden

Plate 38 (left): A freight train of the old order, formed of unfitted and part-fitted goods stock, most of which entered service during the 1950s. In an unfitted train, such as this, air and vacuum-braked stock can be conveyed on the same train, albeit with no brakes working. In this view of Class 40, No. 40081 entering Healey Mills Yard, the first vehicle is an air-braked cement wagon, while the remainder of the train is made up of a mixture of vacuum and unfitted vehicles.

Colin Marsden

Plate 42 (above): The movement of stone from the quarries to regional permanent way yards is usually undertaken using air brake-fitted stone hoppers. Each hopper is often capable of holding up to 50 tons of stone and thus restricts the number of wagons able to be hauled in one train. Class 33 No. 33013 approaches Woking permanent way yard, on 13th November 1979, with a heavy stone train from Westbury.

Colin Marsden

Plate 43 (below): The movement of cars from builders' yards to central distribution points, or from ports to the car company factories for completion, is often carried out on double deck car transporter units which are formed into four vehicle sets with articulated bogies on 'inner vehicles'. An empty train of these 'car-tic' wagons, headed by Class 31 No. 31245, is seen passing Doncaster Works and heading south on 30th October 1980.

Colin Marsden

Plate 44 (left): The modern block freight trains give a pleasing appearance to the eye, with all the vehicles being of the same design and, usually, the same livery. Here, on 9th September 1981, a chemical train, headed by dual-braked Class 40 No. 40086, stops in Skelton Yard, York, after arriving from the north-east. In the background Class 31 No. 31156 comes to a stand with a vacuum brake-fitted long-welded rail train, which is bound for the nearby permanent way yard.

Colin Marsden

Plate 46 (top right): As the whole of the BR main line locomotive fleet is not equipped with train air brake equipment, the diagramming of locomotives to operate air-braked freight services is of paramount importance for the satisfactory running of the operation. The task of ensuring that this is done is placed in the hands of the area control operators. Here Class 40, No. 40131, heads the 14.25 Parkeston Quay—Bathgate ABS train past March on 23rd September 1981.

Barry Nicolle

Plate 45 (left): Areas such as the north-east of the country see considerably more freight traffic than the south-east, and much of this extra traffic is conveyed in British Rail-owned 'Railfreight' wagons. Passing the tall semaphore signals at Norton-on-Tees, Class 37 No. 37020 hauls a lengthy train of empty flats, on 18th May 1982, from Hartlepool towards Thornaby.

Colin Marsden

Plate 47 (right): In the South of England, most of the aggregate road stone used for building work, mainly for motorway construction, is conveyed, from quarries near Westbury, in block air-braked hopper trains, which are usually powered by Class 37, 47 or 56 locomotives. In this view, Class 47 No. 47252 passes Andover while hauling empty hoppers, which are owned by the Amey Roadstone Company, back towards Westbury.

Colin Marsden

Plate 48: Trains to and from the continental ports often convey vehicles not owned by B R. They are owned, either, by one of the foreign railway companies or a foreign freight company, and this was the case, on 3rd September 1981, when Class 40 No. 40057 was photographed passing Wrabness, with the 21.35 Bathgate–Parkeston Quay AB service. The seven vehicles at the rear belong to a continental operator.

Colin Marsden

Plate 49: One of the major oil refineries in the country is situated, on Southampton Water, at Fawley, and much of the oil is transferred from the plant, by underground pipes, to large users such as airports, but a considerable amount is also distributed by rail, usually in block train loads. Class 33 locomotives Nos. 33060 and 33061 head empty 100 tonne G LW tanks near Winchester on 7th July 1981.

Colin Marsden

Plate 50 (above): During the late 1970s and early 1980s it has been the norm for the railway, and also private industry, to produce much larger vehicles — some being able to carry up to 100 tons of goods. For the transport of powdered clay from Cornwall, a fleet of 'Polybulk' AB bogie wagons entered traffic during the mid-1970s. In this illustration, Class 47 No. 47001 heads eleven 'Polybulk' wagons past West Drayton.

Colin Marsden

Plate 51 (below): Many of the larger roadstone companies now operate sizeable fleets of AB hopper wagons, and during the 1980s these could be seen on most regions. The train pictured here is operated by the Redland Group and is seen traversing the 'up' slow line of the Midland main line, at Sharnbrook, on 4th August 1981, headed by Class 45 'Peak' No. 45004.

Colin Marsden

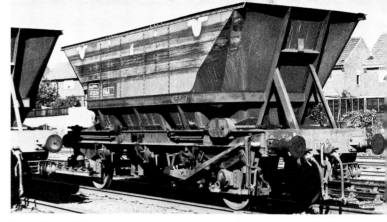

Plate 52 (top left): The largest covered vans currently in operation on the BR network are a fleet of VTG ferry vans, painted in aluminium livery. As can be seen from the end connections, these vehicles are equipped for air brake operation. In addition they have through vacuum pipes which enables them to be formed into trains of vacuum-braked stock, which often becomes necessary when they are moved from one yard to another. It will also be noted that only one air pipe, a brake pipe, is provided, the main air reservoir pipe not being required.

Colin Marsden

Plate 53 (top right): By far the largest single commodity moved in Britain, by rail, is coal. Apart from the existence of many vacuum and non-fitted wagons, there are several thousands of all steel merry-go-round wagons in traffic, all of which are fitted with automatic air brake equipment. Vehicles have floor-mounted doors which, when passed over discharging activators at power-stations, automatically open the doors to discharge the coal on to underground conveyors. No. 353639, built in 1968, shows the general delapidated state of the vehicle bodies after only a short period in use.

Colin Marsden

Plate 54 (above): A substantial fleet of privately-owned bogie cement wagons is in traffic, classified under British Rail's TOPS system as PDA. Normally, these wagons operate in block loads from cement works to consumer. On 5th August 1981, Class 33, No. 33054 was photographed between Wandsworth Town and Clapham Junction, with just two such vehicles in tow, bound for the cement works at Northfleet, Kent.

Colin Marsden

Plate 55 (below): These days, it is very rare to see a new railway open, but on 24th November 1981 a 1¼ mile diversionary route, on the Western Valley line near Rogerstone, was commissioned. This was as a result of Gwent Council's decision to build part of the new Rogerstone—Risca bypass over part of the existing route. The first train to traverse the 'new' line was an air brake-fitted steel train, shown here, headed by Class 37 No. 37185.

Colin Marsden

Plate 56 (above): On the Southern Region, where freight traffic is at a low ebb, commodities transported to and from the ports often involve the use of continental stock hauled by BR locomotives. Headed by Class 73 No. 73128 the train, shown here, is formed entirely of vehicles conforming to the RIV (Continental operating requirement) and is seen passing through the Kent countryside, near Smarden, en route for the docks at Dover.

Colin Marsden

Plate 57 (left): For the conveyance of perishable goods, a daily vans train, normally formed of some 6—10 vehicles, always of air-braked stock and often with a mixture of British and continental-designed vehicles, operates between Dover and the transverser terminal at Paddock Wood. Class 33 No. 33021 is pictured passing Sevington, south of Ashford, Kent, with four continental and two BR 'Railfreight' vehicles.

Colin Marsden

Plate 58 (above): The heaviest trains to operate in this country are air brake-fitted bogie iron ore tippler wagons, that ply between Port Talbot and the BSC works at Llanwern, between Newport and Severn Tunnel Junction. These trains run three or four times each day and are normally formed of 27 rotary tippler wagons, necessitating the use of two Class 56 locomotives or, if not available, three Class 37 locomotives, as a gross trailing weight of 2,740 tons has to be hauled. Here Class 56 locomotives Nos. 56044 and 56041 approach Llanwern on 10th November 1981.

Colin Marsden

Plate 59 (below): Although many of the recently introduced air-braked covered vans look alike, there are no less than nine different types. The differences are found in door sizes and arrangements, whether the vehicle is ventilated, the weight of goods that can be carried and the brake fitting. Some vehicles are supplied with through vacuum pipes in addition to having the continuous air brake. The train shown here, headed by Class 50 No. 50025 *Invincible,* is formed of VDA style wagons which have centre and end doors, are non-ventilated and can carry 25 tons of goods.

Colin Marsden

Plate 60 (above): For many years most coal traffic, in the north-eastern region of the country, was conveyed in unfitted 21 ton coal wagons which dated back to the 1950s. However, from the early 1980s, modern air-braked high capacity coal wagons were introduced, and these now operate some 50 per cent of traffic in the area. A heavily-loaded train, from South Hetton NCB complex, headed by Class 37, No. 37045, is photographed passing Hart Junction, north of Hartlepool, on 18th May 1982.

Colin Marsden

Plate 61 (below): Despite the fact that the majority of freight trains in Devon and Cornwall are of the air-braked type, an occasional vacuum-braked train operates. In this view, Class 47 No. 47331 passes Tavistock Junction with a train of vacuum-braked stock bound for South Wales. The second vehicle in the train is a modern air-fitted van, but with a through vacuum pipe enabling it to work in this train, albeit without brakes in operation.

Colin Marsden

Plate 62 (right): As previously mentioned, the largest user of the air-braked freight system, for the movement of large quantities of coal from the pits to its large users, such as the Central Electricity Generating Board (CEGB), is the National Coal Board. The section of line between Beighton Junction and Worksop sees something in excess of 95 air-fitted merry-go-round trains each day. Passing the now-closed, and demolished, signal box at Kiveton Park Station, Class 31 locomotives Nos. 31147 and 31235 haul a heavy train from the nearby colliery on 30th January 1980.

Colin Marsden

Plate 63 (below): At the eastern extremities of the Worksop—Beighton line are the large CEGB power-stations of Cottam and West Burton and, between them, these account for some 60 trains per day. Each train is normally formed of 32 wagons and each wagon is able to convey 32½ tons of coal. Class 56 locomotives are normally used for these workings and No. 56058 is seen here, on 10th September 1981, passing Kiveton Park whilst heading back to the pits from West Burton.

Colin Marsden

Plate 64: Train arrivals at the CEGB power-station at Eggborough, near Whitley Bridge, are at almost hourly intervals throughout the day and night, and one of the main sources of coal for this station is the nearby Kellingley Colliery. On 11th September 1981, Class 56 No. 56074 is shown here arriving on the CEGB tracks at Eggborough from the colliery. The roof light on the locomotive is for a remote control system used in the power-station.

Colin Marsden

Plate 66 (above): Coal from NCB pits in the Barrow Hill area, for West Burton or Cottam power-stations, usually have to run round in the yards near Woodhouse Station, thus making Woodhouse an ideal place for enthusiasts to see merry-go-round trains. Class 56 No. 56075 stands in the yard, after arrival from Bolsover Colliery, prior to running round, while Class 47 No. 47316 passes with a vacuum-fitted ballast train. Two other loaded merry-go-round trains can be seen awaiting departure.

Colin Marsden

Plate 67 (below): The supply of locomotives for power-station workings, in the Ferrybridge, Eggborough and Drax areas, is looked after by the small diesel depot and wagon repair work, which is conveniently situated, on the Leeds—Goole line, at Knottingley. Class 56 locomotives Nos. 56032 and 56012, and a Class 08 shunter No. 08243, stand in the shed yard on 11th September 1981. At weekends, up to 15 main line locomotives can be found on shed.

Colin Marsden

Plate 65 (left): With a man-made mountain of coal slag visible on the horizon, Class 56 No. 56035 passes Featherstone, on 11th September 1981, on the freight only Crofton Junction—Pontefract line, with a loaded merry-go-round train bound for Ferrybridge Power-Station. The train probably originated from one of the nearby mechanized pits.

Colin Marsden

Plate 68 (top left):   In the foreseeable future, it is the British Railway Board's intention to do away with guards working on these block air brake-fitted trains, as their job is now practically irrelevant with very little work to do, except for keeping a watchful eye on the following train. With modern TOPS controlled yards, the guard does not have to take wagon numbers, and train preparation and calculation is carried out by depot staff with the aid of a computer. Class 56 No. 56024 passes Pontefract Monkhill, during late 1981, while bound for Drax Power-Station.

Colin Marsden

Plate 69 (bottom left):   Further economic steps in BR manning agreements, will be the removal of the secondman or driver's assistant, leaving the train solely in the control of the driver. This style of fully-fitted single man operated train is already in use on the continent, and will probably occur in this country in the foreseeable future. No. 56024 passes Knottingley, during the late summer of 1981, with a Drax bound train.

Colin Marsden

Plate 70 (above):   One of the latest areas to see Class 56 operation, on air-braked hopper wagons, is in the north-east, on Blyth Power-Station workings. These trains are formed of the most modern HBA style hopper wagons, rather than the time honoured HAA type. A loaded train is seen here, on 20th May 1982, headed by Class 56 No. 56077, passing Newcastle Central and bound for Blyth.

Colin Marsden

HIGH SPEED DEVELOPMENT

The story of high speed development can really be traced back as far as the autumn of 1935, when the LNER instigated a fast service, between Newcastle and King's Cross, formed of streamlined air-smoothed stock hauled by an 'A4' class 4-6-2 steam locomotive. This new, prestigious, service, named 'Silver Jubilee', covered the 268½ miles in 3½ hours, giving an average speed of 65.8mph. During the following years, various railway companies also introduced special limited stop services on their more important routes, thus giving a far improved service to the public.

After railway nationalization, in January 1948, the new BR fleet of main line steam locomotives was wide and varied, with many of the larger locomotives being capable of prolonged fast running at speeds of up to 90/100mph. Prior to nationalization, the LMS, at their Derby Works, had constructed two diesel-electric medium power range Co-Co locomotives, and it was decided that future high speed development should be concentrated in this field.

During the BR modernization plan of the mid-1950s, various batches of diesel locomotives, of various power outputs, were ordered, but still the maximum permitted road speed was only 90mph. The magic 100mph mark was not authorized for a fleet of main line diesel locomotives until the BR Type 5 'Deltic' locomotive, later Class 55, was constructed, during the early 1960s, by English Electric. It was soon found, on proving trials and service running, that speeds well in excess of 100mph could be, and indeed were, obtained from these 3,300hp locomotives.

The next major step towards the advancement of the diesel engine, and eventual high speed running, was during 1967 when a fleet of fifty English Electric-built, but BR-designed, locomotives was ordered for sustained 100mph running on the northern sections of the London Midland Region. These Type 4 locomotives, later designated Class 50, were fitted with the same basic design English Electric diesel engine that was fitted in the LMS-designed locomotives, Nos. 10000 and 10001 in 1947/48, but in this, its latest, form giving some 50 per cent greater power output.

For some years the English Electric Company had been experimenting with sophisticated electronic and control systems, which had been fitted into the English Electric trial locomotive, DP2. These included automatic tractive effort control, dynamic braking, inertia air filtration and slow speed control. When the Class 50s were constructed, all this equipment was, for the first time, fitted into a main line production run locomotive, with the idea of eventually improving the traction performance/reliability and speed of the locomotive. Over the years, as time has come to prove, many of these complicated items have been removed; a subject covered in greater detail in the section dealing with Class 50 refurbishment.

BR's quest for higher speed and, therefore, greater efficiency, continued during the 1960s when a significant decision on the future of Britain's main line railways had to be taken. This was whether, like many of the continental railway entities, BR should point large proportions of its resources into building new railways or whether modernization of existing equipment should be carried out to enable higher speed running, of up to 125mph, on existing tracks. During 1966 it was decided to opt for the latter, whereafter considerable research was undertaken into rolling stock technology, so as to produce a train capable of travelling at a higher speed without large scale changes to the present track and signalling systems. Two options

were, therefore, laid open to the planning/design sections:

(a) That of a train based on conventional power/control designs be constructed and fitted into a shell of basically established design;

(b) A train powered from the 25kV a.c. (overhead) be built using new unproven systems, including the use of a coach tilting mechanism.

The first option enabled the train to run on existing tracks at increased speeds of up to 125mph, but when curved sections were encountered speed restrictions had to be imposed. The second option, of a train with a tilting system, enabled the train to take curves at far higher speeds and, on routes such as London to Glasgow, large time scale advantages could be achieved. The BRB had to decide which to choose and, after much prolonged negotiation, it was decided to invest in both systems. Plan A became the high speed diesel project (HST), and Plan B the Advanced Passenger Train project (APT).

In both spheres of design, prototype products had to be built. For the HST design work two power cars, classified as individual locomotives and classed as 41, were constructed by BREL at their Crewe Works, together with a rake of modern air-smoothed Mk III coaches. Power was provided, in each power car, by a Paxman Valenta 12 cylinder 12RP200L diesel engine which gave electric power, via a generator, to four Brush traction motors which were mounted under both ends of each power car. Running and proving trials were carried out on both Eastern and Western regions. The success of this train was such that, during its two year exhaustive testing period, a new world speed record, of 143mph, for diesel traction was achieved. Following on from the Class 41 diesel locomotive set, which was later classified as 252, came the production Class 253 units for the Western Region, and in 1977 the Class 254 sets for the Eastern and Scottish regions.

During the development work from Classes 252 to 253/4, several substantial alterations were carried out, namely in external design of the power cars and certain control equipment and, of course, the livery. The Paxman power plant was retained but traction equipment was provided by GEC Traction Limited. After early teething troubles both classes settled down well to long hard running, and they now have a reliability of over 80 per cent.

Much of the equipment for the APT project was to be totally new to railway operation, and the tilting system was only, to date, a paper project. In 1968 the BRB and MOT invested large sums of money on three major APT associated projects:

(1) To build a gas turbine-powered APT fitted with the tilting coach system (APT—E).

(2) To design and build a laboratory at Derby for APT design and testing.

(3) To test the experimental APT under simulated and actual road conditions.

A four coach gas turbine-powered unit (APT—E) was constructed at Derby Technical Centre. Each power car, one at each end, was driven by four Leyland 350 automotive gas turbines, rated at 298hp, which provided the power for the GEC traction motors. After the train was completed and thoroughly 'on works' tested, it was transferred to the, then, recently acquired test track between Melton Mowbray and Edwalton, on the former Midland Railway route to Nottingham. Here considerable controlled testing was performed prior to the unit running test trips on both London

Midland and Western region metals. One of the principle areas where considerable research had to be carried out was on the coach tilting equipment. The main consideration that had to be taken into account was that even when a maximum tilt, 9 degrees from the vertical, was encountered the train or coach remained within the standard C1 loading gauge. To meet this requirement the designed body had to be much narrower than the conventional-hauled stock currently in use. The sensing devices, or probes, to activate the tilting system were mounted on each coach, which in turn operated that coach's cant survo system. This system was heavily modified on the production electric Class 370 sets. The cant responses had to be rapid as with a train approaching a curve at 125+mph, time scales were only very small, and a basis of 5 degrees per second was worked on.

From the maze of mechanical and computerized information received from the Railway Technical Centre, and 'in traffic' testing laboratories on the APT—E train, the basic prototype passenger carrying trains (APT—P) were constructed. Each set comprised a DTS (Driving Trailer Second), TS (Trailer Second), TRSB (Trailer Restaurant Second Buffet), TU (Trailer Unclassified), TF (Trailer First), TBF (Trailer Brake First), and M (Motor), this giving half a service train formation. The basic appearance was quite different from the APT—E train, with the main power plant now being incorporated in the middle of the formation. The external contours of the vehicles were basically the same as the 'E' train, but considerable front end redesigning was carried out. One of the reasons for this was the requirement for the fitting of a buffing gear system, which, if the need arose, enabled the train to be hauled. As well as fitting the main electric power plant in the centre of a train formation, auxiliary low-powered diesel engines were installed just behind the cab sections of DTS vehicles. The 9 degrees cant system installed in the 'E' train was heavily modified and fitted to the 'P' formation, but considerable design work had still to be carried out on the power car cant system, as the roof-mounted pantographs could not be allowed to move 9 degrees from the vertical or damage would result. To alleviate this problem a complicated pantograph anti-tilt mechanism, with direct linkage between the bogies and pantograph, was devised. After the power coaches had been constructed at Derby, road testing was carried out but, at the time, few vehicles of the actual APT—P train were ready for 'on road' testing. A special train was made up and consisted of the former power cars of the prototype Class 252 HST with an assortment of test and recording vehicles. From early 1979, when sufficient APT vehicles were completed, most of the testing work was transferred to Glasgow Shields Road Depot or Derby RTC for minor rectification and modification. Continuing through 1979 it became a part of the scene in the north-west, regularly running at 125+ mph. On 20th December 1979, during one set of trials, the maximum recorded speed was 160mph. Throughout 1980 and 1981 high speed testing of various train formations was conducted, which culminated in much redesign and modification work being carried out, including alterations to the cant sensing systems.

Some people would perhaps say that now a train capable of running at 125mph over conventional track has been produced, the 'high speed development' has come near to an end, but, alas, this is not the case, and in the design offices at London and Derby plans are being made for an even faster age of railway travel.

Plates 71 to 73: During the mid-1960s, the British Railway's design panel were hard at work producing various external body designs for trains of the future. In the upper and centre plates, two early Advanced Passenger Train variants are shown, both with the articulated bogies on trailer vehicles. Although, in the initial stages, a rounded front end was favoured, this was later replaced by a semi-flat front end built into the prototype gas turbine-powered unit. In the lower plate is the initial mock-up of the diesel-electric high speed diesel train set, showing, even at this early stage, in 1969, that vehicles of a non-articulated type were envisaged. Although production vehicles differed, much of their design can be traced back to this mock-up. The centre coupling is exposed on this mock-up, whereas on the production fleet it was placed under a housing and, of course, headlights and marker lights replaced the headcode system which, in the 1960s, was still in use.

British Railways

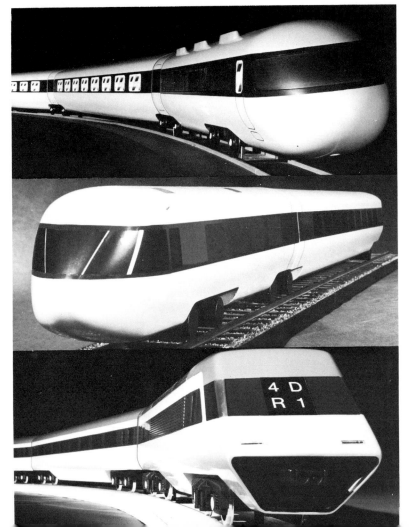

Plate 74 (above): Following the decision to build a full-sized passenger carrying prototype HST, Crewe Works was given the job of co[n]structing the power cars while Derby Works carried out the construction of intermediate coaches. Pictured here, inside the main erecti[ng] shop at Crewe Works, is the body frame of car No. 1 of HST production, which is standing awaiting the fitting of equipment and bo[dy] panelling.

British Railwa[ys]

Plate 75 (below): The finished product. The first High Speed Train power car stands outside Crewe Works after completion, and [is] carrying locomotive running number 41001. The livery applied was that of the BR Pullman; grey with a blue band at window heig[ht] and full yellow warning ends. The head and marker lights were positioned behind a glass front panel, which was a continuation of t[he] driver's window panel. Although the vehicle was intended, when in operation, to be driven from the leading end only, a set of 'bas[ic]' controls was provided in the guard's compartment for running light, a feature not continued in the production vehicles.

Colin Marso[n]

Plate 76 (right): The Research and Development Section at Derby played an important part in the construction of the two power cars, and worked closely with the BREL team at Crewe. Actual cab sections were fabricated in the plastics laboratory, at Derby, and here a buffer skirt is being fitted to the monocoque reinforced plastic/foam sandwich-constructed cab and nose module of a power car. In the foreground one of the component moulds can be seen.

British Railways

Plate 77 (below): When initially placed into traffic, the unit operated on the Eastern Region and was based at Leeds Neville Hill Depot, but by 1975 it was the turn of the Western Region to evaluate the train and give their customers a foretaste of future rail travel. When first used on the Western Region, the only route passed for operation was between Paddington and Weston-super-Mare, and it was on this line, on 4th July 1975, that the unit was photographed. It will be noted that the set was carrying 'unit' No. 252001 in place of individual locomotive numbers.

Barry Nicolle

Plate 78 (above): Once the HST was in traffic, on the Western Region, much public relations work took place in gauging passenger reaction to various aspects of the train. Initially, due to operating difficulties, the set was restricted to 100mph in passenger traffic, with 125mph operation commencing at the end of 1976. The unit is seen here, pulling out of Bristol Temple Meads, on 16th June 1975, on a Paddington—Weston-super-Mare working.

Graham Scott-Lowe

Plate 79 (below): Extensive test running, using the prototype HST driving cars, occurred during 1976, once the initial order for production vehicles was in traffic. Coupled to Derby CM&EE test car No. 6, ADB975290, formerly FK No. S13396, the prototype Class 252 motor car stands at Swindon, during June 1976, while undergoing high speed running trials between Old Oak Common and Bristol.

Brian Morrison

Test Car 6

Plate 80 (right): Between 1976 and 1982 the production shops at BREL Crewe Works undertook construction of 198 HST power cars, which were estimated to be worth in the region of £50 million. From the laying of frames to the trials of the car was about 12 weeks. The final power car to be constructed, No. 43198, is shown here, on 6th April 1982, soon after arriving, in the erecting shop, from the fabrication shop. In this shop the body panels were affixed and general construction commenced.

Colin Marsden

Plate 81 (below): Whilst the power cars were under construction at Crewe, the trailer passenger carrying vehicles were built at Derby, Litchurch Lane, Carriage Works. A row of finished coaches is seen here awaiting painting. Construction of each vehicle took about 12 weeks and up to 30 vehicles could be under assembly at one time.

British Railways

Plate 84 (above): After the introduction of IC125 sets on the Western Region, the Eastern and Scottish regions were next in line to operate them. Sets were allocated to Bounds Green in London, Leeds (Neville Hill) and Newcastle (Heaton) and, following the introduction of the trains through to Edinburgh, an allocation was given to Craigentinny. Set No. 254007 races past Tuxford, on 23rd April 1981, with a northbound train.

Colin Marsden

Plate 85 (right): Unlike the Western Region, where unit formations remain constant, on Eastern and Scottish regions unit variations are found, some having 2 buffet cars, others only one, and some may also have an additional TS coach. These different formations depend on the routes which the units are intended to work over. The set shown here, passing Gamston, to the south of Retford, is formed of two first, two buffets and four second class vehicles.

Colin Marsden

Plate 86 (above): After the initial introduction of sets on the Bristol and South Wales route of the Western Region, the next operating area to receive units, to replace locomotive-hauled trains, was between Paddington and Penzance. To cater for this extension to the network, a new IC125 train servicing depot was built adjacent to Laira Depot, in Plymouth, which enabled maintenance to be carried out on sets being used on the London route as well as the north-east/south-west 'Heartline' service. On 27th June 1980, set No. 253036 is pictured passing Brent, in South Devon, with the 12.03 service from Penzance to Paddington.

Colin Marsden

Plate 87 (below): The booked formation of Western Region sets, in use on the London services, is 1 TGS (Trailer Guards Second), 3 TS (Trailer Seconds), 1 TRUB/TRSB (Trailer Restaurant Unclassified Buffet/Trailer Restaurant Second Buffet) and 2 FO (First Opens), giving a total train loading of 96 first and 314 second class seats. Set No. 253028 slowly departs from Bristol Temple Meads with the 13.20 Paddington—Plymouth service on 2nd June 1981.

Colin Marsden

Plate 88 (right): Although IC125 sets are designed for 125mph operation, it is not possible to attain this speed at a number of locations and, at the present time, this speed is not permitted west of Exeter. Nevertheless, with the use of such trains on the Paddington—Penzance route, a saving of 23 minutes can be made, although this effectively reduces the number of seats available by 25 per cent. Passing the now-closed station of Brent, on 15th June 1981, is the 12.25 Paddington—Plymouth train.
Colin Marsden

Plate 89 (below): Following the full introduction of the IC125 sets, from the autumn of 1982, when Laira took delivery of its final set for use on the north-east/south-west route, at the time of writing, little further advance in high speed passenger service can be seen in the foreseeable future. However, further time saving would be possible where major track working is projected, raising the maximum pemitted speed. On the Eastern Region it is unlikely that any great change in passenger trends will occur, or that much reduction in travelling times will be gained during the remainder of the 1980s. An Eastern Region set, led by power car No. 43101, approaches Doncaster with the 06.47 Newcastle—King's Cross service on 23rd April 1981.

Colin Marsden

Plate 90 (above): Concurrent with the building of the proto-type high speed diesel train, the engineers, at Derby Technical Centre, built the four coach experimental Advanced Passenger Train (APT—E). Trailer cars and the inner ends of the power cars were mounted on articulated bogies and access was via plug doors above the bogies. This gas turbine-powered unit operated under trial conditions on various routes, and engineers and scientists gained much knowledge on high speed running and, more importantly, on the tilt system which was incorporated, for the first time, in a train in this country. This photograph shows the APT—E standing, when new, outside Derby Technical Centre.

British Railways

Plate 91 (below): After it was decided to opt for an electric APT, design and construction work was concentrated at Derby, and various vehicles were built during the mid-1970s. Here, two of the mammoth power cars stand awaiting atten-tion in the Derby Locomotive Works yard. Each power car houses electrical equipment capable of developing 4,000 h p.

Colin Marsden

Plate 92 (above): After the introduction, during 1978/79, of pre-production electric APT units, considerable testing was carried out, and much of this involved the tilt mechanism and traction equipment and, although each 'train' was designed to operate with two power cars, for much of the testing odd combinations were to be seen. For an extended trial period Glasgow Shields Road Depot became the home of these units and it is here, during 1980, that sets Nos. 370004 and 370006 are seen.

Tom Noble

Plate 93 (below): Painted in distinctive grey, black and red livery, APT No. 370001 heads down the West Coast Main Line during running trials. Although originally designed for a maximum speed of 150 mph, it was decided that the maximum speed in passenger service would be 125 mph, although trials in excess of 150 mph have been satisfactorily achieved.

British Railways

RAIL OPERATIONS BY NIGHT

Most observers who follow British Railways' operations, usually only study those which are undertaken during the day. In this short feature, we look at the variety of railway operations that take place at night and the many types of train not normally observed by the daytime onlooker.

One of the largest operations by night is the transportation of mail for the GPO. For this service a large fleet of TPO (Travelling Post Office) trains operate on all regions, thereby linking major towns and cities. To supplement this fleet, many hundreds of ordinary van trains operate throughout the railway, conveying mail and parcel traffic loaded by GPO staff at the originating station and collected by their staff at its destination. Trains formed of TPO vehicles usually set out on their journey between 20.00 and 23.30 hrs to enable arrival at their destination in time for letters to be delivered by first post the following morning. In some areas where, by virtue of use and loading requirements, van or mail trains do not operate, mail bags are either loaded into the guard's van of passenger trains, or on to a special train, comprising passenger stock, which is run entirely for mail purposes.

A night contract, which the railway has operated for many years, is for the conveyance of newspapers from the major printing cities of London, Manchester and Glasgow. The products of all printing houses are loaded on to one train, and sorting and packaging takes place en route. For this service the railway operates a fleet of converted BG, GUV and PVG vans fitted with internal tables, and on PVG type vehicles washing facilities are also provided.

So as not to interfere with daytime passenger services, a large number of freight trains operate by night, and during recent years, with the introduction of 'Speedlink' and other such services, night operations have largely increased.

'Speedlink' trains, that are loaded during the day in private sidings or BR terminals, set out for their destination at pre-timetabled times and are either delivered to company sidings or are available at a local railhead the following day.

In general, during the early 1980s, parcels traffic on the BR system has been greatly reduced, with, now, only a handful of trains still operating.

Many passenger services operate at night with local services on some inner city and suburban routes, and Inter-City sleepers and conventional main line services on others. The comfort of the Inter-City sleepers has, with the introduction, in 1982, of Mk III sleeping vehicles, greatly improved. In some areas all night passenger services operate, and one of the most famous is between London Victoria and Gatwick Airport where an hourly service is provided.

At night, when services are very sparse, the railway can make good use of the opportunity to maintain locomotives and vehicles at their many depots around the system. Stock and traction units are often taken out of service at the close of the day, given extensive maintenance overnight, and returned to traffic the following morning.

The Civil Engineering Department also have to make good use of slack operational periods, and on most nights of the year, permanent way track possessions for relaying, re-railing and general track maintenance, including track tamping and lining, takes place.

Plate 94: After the majority of passengers have gone home for the night, the railway has to move empty stock around the system in readiness for the next day's services. Class 50 No. 50043 *Eagle* stands at Exeter, on 15th September 1982, with empty stock from Westbury to Plymouth.

Colin Marsden

Plate 95 (above right): When most people think of rail operations at night, they envisage a few passenger trains formed of sleeping car stock, but this is not the case and a large proportion of other traffic is in operation at night. On each region a large quantity of mail is transported by rail and, where heavy loadings prevail, special travelling post office trains operate. A train formed of three TPO vehicles headed by Class 45 'Peak' No. 45137, *The Bedfordshire and Hertfordshire Regiment (T.A.),* waits to depart from Derby during the evening of 30th January 1980.

Colin Marsden

Plate 95a (below right): There are two types of vehicle in traffic for the conveyance of mail by rail. One fleet is classified as POS (Post Office Sorters), and these vehicles are equipped with sorting trays and letter racks. Mail, from Post Offices and post boxes, is taken directly into these vehicles and sorted into areas whilst the train is in motion. The other fleet is classified as POT (Post Office Tender) and mail bags are stored in these vehicles until they are required, for sorting, in the POS vehicle. POS No. S80379 is shown in this photograph.

Colin Marsden

Plate 96 (above): It is usually arranged that travelling Post Office trains leave their originating point after the last main collection of the day, but allowing sufficient time to arrive at their destination in time for the first delivery the following morning. The Penzance–Paddington postal, shown here headed by Class 50 No. 50015 *Valiant*, departs from Penzance at 19.27 and arrives at Paddington at 03.50.

Colin Marsden

Plate 97 (below): Perhaps some customers would wonder if their mail would ever reach its destination, if they saw this mound of mail bags at York, in the early hours of 15th February 1982, waiting to be loaded on to a southbound overnight service to King's Cross. Each mail bag carries a destination label, or identification of the station at which it is to be detrained, and if the bag has to change trains en route, this is also labelled to avoid delay.

Ian Gould

Plate 98 (above): In some suburban areas, local passenger units are used to form special mail or parcels trains, and this often occurs during the early evening period. Southern Region Class 405, (4SUB) No. 4639, stands in the bay platform at Twickenham on a wet 6th October 1981, and forms the 19.26 Waterloo—Waterloo (via Kingston upon Thames) parcels and mail train.

Colin Marsden

te 99 (right): Other night users the rail network, for the con- ance of newspapers from ndon to the major conurbations the country, are the large print ses. Special fleets of GUV, BG PVG vehicles used for this pose, are usually labelled wspapers' and are equipped h internal sorting tables. The t of PVG vans was converted ing the early 1980s and are ed with washing facilities for paper sorting staff. The 01.40 terloo—Yeovil, headed by Class No. 33016, awaits departure m Waterloo on 30th March 31. The first vehicle behind the omotive is a BG.

Colin Marsden

Plate 100 (left): Most of the larger London stations have carriage yards, in close proximity where the stock used overnight can be observed during the day. Outside Waterloo, the yards at Clapham Junction provide the storage space for all stock used from the terminal. Class 73 No. 73137 waits, in Clapham Junction Yard with empty stock for Waterloo, to form one of the overnight services to Bournemouth.

Colin Marsden

Plate 101 (below): At the beginning of the 1980s there were several thousand locomotive hauled vans being used to convey parcel traffic, but by the end of 1982, only a handful remained, and most of these are scheduled for withdrawal in the next few years. The general decline in parcels traffic, and the transfer to road haulage, are the main reasons for this change of operation. Class 33 No. 33046 stands at Guildford with the daily 20.13 Maidstone–Reading vans service. Trains such as this are more easily pathed by night when passenger traffic is at a low level.

Andrew French

Plate 102 (above): On the Western and Midland regions a small fleet of diesel parcels vans operate on local traffic, during the day as well as at night, but they are more often seen during the evening and night period. On the Southern Region a fleet of electric single cars operate for parcels traffic and are used in conjunction with electric multiple unit sets. Western Region allocated car No. W55991 stands at Paddington on 10th November 1981.

Colin Marsden

Plate 103 (below): A typical sight, seen by thousands of travellers every day and night; the PMV (Parcels and Miscellaneous Van). These vehicles were built, between 1938 and 1942, to Southern Railway design, and can carry some 10 tons of goods. The majority of parcels trains seen in service will have at least one of these vehicles in its formation. Although they are of Southern origin, they can be seen today, at all points around the network. No. S1792 stands at Bristol Temple Meads.

Colin Marsden

Plate 104 (above): Much of the nation wide freight system of 'Railfreight' and 'Speedlink' services operate during the hours of darkness, after closure of business for many of the manufacturing industries. Class 40 No. 40081 stands awaiting a relief driver, at Doncaster, with a Tyne Yard bound 'Railfreight' on a cold evening in September 1981.

Colin Marsden

Plate 105 (left): At Stratford, London is the LIFT (London International Freight Terminal). Much activity takes place at night in loading and unloading trains of produce that has either arrived from the continent, or is on its way, in refrigerated or ventilated vans, to one of the European countries. A French ferry van is waiting to be loaded outside one of the large sheds and will soon be despatched, via the rail ferry at Harwich, to the continent.

Colin Marsden

Plate 106 (right): If a study of the passenger timetable is made, it will be noted that passenger services, on many routes, operate throughout the night, or commence at a very early hour. Night trains are often provided near the large motive power depots to provide a service for train crews signing on and off duty. Three car Class 116 set No. C318 stands at Cardiff Central Station, in the early hours of 3rd November 1981.

Ian Gould

Plate 107 (left): Train services from the big cities usually operate until midnight in order to transport late night travellers. On a damp January evening, two Eastern Region diesel multiple unit sets stand at Sheffield Station. The set on the right, with car No. E56002 leading, awaits departure to Leeds with the last train of the day.

Colin Marsden

Plate 108 (below): Although services on the Crewe—Cardiff route do not operate throughout the night, in winter months the 19.25 service traverses the complete length of the line under cover of darkness. On 3rd October 1981, the 19.25 is ready to depart, and is formed of a rake of Mk I stock and headed by Class 33 No. 33001.

Colin Marsden

Plate 109 (left): A major advance for night travellers in the 1980s came early in 1982 when the first of the Mk III new generation of sleeping cars came into service on the Eastern Region. The new vehicles are fully air-conditioned and were constructed with hindsight of the Taunton sleeping car fire tragedy. Each vehicle is now equipped with smoke detectors and an alarm system. Class 47 No. 47434 stands at the head of the 22.15 night 'Aberdonian' at King's Cross on 4th June 1982.

Colin Marsden

Plate 110 (below): An improvement in the new Mk III sleeping car stock is that each vehicle can be arranged to accommodate either first or second class passengers. When laid out for second class occupation, two berths are provided, but when in use as first class accommodation, the upper berth is stowed away to give more room in the rather cramped compartment. Prior to entering revenue earning service, several test runs took place, between Aberdeen and King's Cross, and pictured here is a test train, headed by a Class 47 locomotive, standing at Dundee Station at the end of 1981.

C. P. Boocock

Plate 111 (above): To achieve a full availability of main line locomotives during the day, much maintenance has to be undertaken overnight, and at most depots a three shift staff roster is worked. The light burns late in this view of Bristol Bath Road Depot, on 10th November 1981, with a Class 33 locomotive receiving attention after arriving with the last train from Portsmouth. Classes 47, 31 and 45 are all used for night duties on many freight and passenger workings in the Bristol area.

Colin Marsden

Plate 112 (right): Class 50 No. 50001 *Dreadnought* stands in the servicing shed at Plymouth (Laira) after a hard day at work. It is usual policy for a locomotive to receive a service check of oil, fuel and water, and then return to traffic. However, if any defects are found the locomotive will be taken out of service and receive urgent attention, as a non-productive locomotive is lost revenue to B R.

Brian Morrison

NEW LOCOMOTIVE BUILDING

After the large numbers of locomotives introduced as a direct result of the 1955 modernization plan, and a handful of others emerging during the early 1960s, the most up to date diesel locomotive introduced, prior to 1976, was the fleet of fifty English Electric Type 4s. These were later designated Class 50, and were independently built under BR guidelines during 1967/68.

In the early 1970s when the quest for higher speed was being made, the railway's own workshops at Crewe produced two locomotive units which were to be the power plant for the, then, new and projected high speed train system, and this subject is covered, in more depth, in the section High Speed Development.

The first major locomotive construction to be undertaken since 1968 was the Class 56. During the mid-1970s the fleets of BR freight and mixed traffic locomotives were not in a very healthy state, and with many potential heavy and long distance freight train contracts foreseen, particularly with coal in the north-east and Midlands, some drastic traction policies had to be taken.

Two possibilities were open to the Board:

(a) to undertake extensive and potentially costly conversion work on existing traction units, or

(b) design and construct, quickly, a new heavy freight locomotive.

It was decided that the second option was the most economical on a long term basis, and tenders, for the construction, within the BREL group, together with certain foreign locomotive builders, were sought. The BREL group would have been awarded the complete contract but, due to the projected delivery date, given by BREL, being basically unacceptable to the British Railways Board, a contract was drawn up for the first thirty locomotives to be built by Brush Electrical Machines (BEM) at a works in Romania. A production clause in the contract was that completed locomotives would be despatched to Britain on a time scale set by BR, and transferred, via the Zeebrugge—Harwich ferry, in a 'ready to run' condition.

The first locomotive, carrying BR running number 56001, and painted in British Rail's corporate blue and yellow livery, operated running and proving trials in Romania prior to being delivered to Zeebrugge, during July 1976, for despatch to the United Kingdom. After arrival at Harwich, an immediate inspection was carried out prior to the locomotive being hauled 'dead' to a new home at Tinsley, near Sheffield, where a further detailed inspection took place. The locomotive then undertook acceptance running with a fixed load train. All the Brush Electrical fleet were delivered and operational by October 1977, by which time further batches of Class 56 locomotives were already under construction at BREL Doncaster, and their first production locomotive, No. 56031, was already at an advanced stage of construction.

Little is known of the construction timetable and procedure in Romania, but Doncaster Works is a little less secretive about its production and a brief timetable is given below.

Stage 1: Frame formed in fabrication shop, and body sides panelled. After completion here, body shell, mounted on trolley bogies (former Class 24 power bogies), is fitted with temporary draw gear for transfer between shops.

Stage 2: From the fabrication shop the shell is transported to the paint shop where pre-assembly shell painting takes place. From here, still mounted on the temporary trolley bogies but now lime green in colour, the shell is taken to the new build shop (E2).

Stage 3: After arrival in E2 shop the trolley bogies are removed and returned to the fabrication shop for re-use. Now mounted on shop stands, the general fitting out and body construction begins. This process normally takes about 13 weeks. When the locomotive emerges, it is bodily complete but not, as yet, passed for operation. After removal from E2 shop and now mounted on its own power bogies, the locomotive passes to Stage 4.

Stage 4: The flash test booth (part of the locomotive paint shop), where insulation breakdown tests are carried out using high amperage shore supply current. If these tests prove successful, the locomotive is now ready to be started up and placed under controlled test conditions.

Stage 5: Whilst being tested the locomotive is run up in the works yard, and also in the test house, to ascertain that all components are functioning correctly, and so any necessary adjustments can be made. If any major faults arise at this stage, the locomotive is returned to E2 shop for rectification.

At this point in the construction programme, depending on paint shop commitments, the locomotive will receive a full paint and cosmetic attention. This is done prior to the locomotive being finally handed over to the works CM&EE Department for main line trial running, which normally consists of a merry-go-round train to and from the Scunthorpe area. If testing proves to be 100 per cent satisfactory, the completed locomotive is then despatched to its allocated R&M Depot.

During the mid-1970s, the Class 56 design was further developed, both in body and technical specification and, therefore, many modifications have been incorporated, at various intervals, throughout the build.

In the mid-1970s, the BR design panel was engaged on planning the next generation of main line diesel traction to follow the Class 56, and in 1977/78 plans were passed for the construction of Class 58 heavy freight locomotives, which were contrived from the Class 56 design. A completely new body design, with external walkways along each side of the locomotive, but retaining the full width driver's cab, was proposed. The power unit, incorporated as the prime mover, was of the same type as that fitted in Class 56s, but formed of 12 cylinders instead of 16, but still capable of producing the same power output of 3,250hp.

The construction of these locomotives was of the modular method, a system, new to BR locomotive building, which was adopted because it was thought to achieve better use of workshop space and available manpower. Each major component, i.e., underframe, cab, coolant group, engine, electrical equipment, etc., could be constructed in different shops and then brought together only in the final construction stage. This system would also achieve a fast turn-round when collision damaged locomotives needed to return to main works for repair, and as all components are of identical design, a 'one off — one on' system could be adopted. From the early design stage it was announced that an export potential, for the Class 58 design, could be envisaged but, regrettably, no firm foreign contracts have yet been secured.

Doncaster Works was chosen to undertake the Class 58 construction, which involved the complete re-tooling of their fabrication and new build shops. Frame fabrication commenced during the summer of 1981 and, by spring of 1982, three frames and many components had been assembled. Only two of the three frames built were actually assembled into locomotives straight away, the third being sent to Derby RTC for stress and strain testing, not returning to Doncaster until late in 1982, for construction in 1983. By the time the third frame had been fabricated, a firm contract, for thirty five locomotives, had been secured which ensured that BREL Doncaster's new build work would continue for the foreseeable future.

As Doncaster had been awarded the Class 58 contract, the construction of the final twenty Class 56 locomotives, Nos. 56116 to 56135, was handed to BREL Crewe, and the frame of No. 56116 was laid at Crewe during January 1982 and, before the year was out, ten engines were in an advanced stage of construction. The initial method of construction, at Crewe, varied slightly from that adopted by Doncaster. When the frame was fabricated, the skin of the body was not applied and only a skeleton frame was assembled prior to general construction work commencing. For the first Crewe built Class 56, the cab sections, and other major components, were supplied en bloc from Doncaster, but Crewe subsequently undertook all major component construction.

The major new build work, carried out at Crewe Works from 1974 until July 1982, was the construction of Inter-City 125 or High Speed diesel train power cars. In 1971, the Works produced two Class 41, later 252, motor vehicles for the prototype HST set which paved the way for the eventual construction of nearly 200 production vehicles of the same basic design, now forming Classes 253 and 254. The IC125 train system is covered in more detail in another section of this book and only the actual production is dealt with here.

Like the Class 56s previously described, each power car starts its life as sheet, girder and fabricated steel. In the fabrication shop all underframe, side support and draw gear assembly are formed into the basic body. From here the body passes to the paint shop for pre-assembly painting, prior to being admitted to the main erecting shop. Here all items, including the main cab assembly which has already been constructed in glass-reinforced plastic in another shop, are progressively fitted. Following main assembly, the car is flash-tested for insulation breakdown before being taken to the paint shop for external finishing. The final 'on works' stage is a short session at the works testing station before undertaking road trials. This is normally carried out with a pair of power cars coupled back to back.

Whilst construction and testing of the power cars has been carried out at Crewe, the intermediate passenger vehicles have been under construction at BREL, Litchurch Lane, Derby. The assembly of coaches is performed in basically the same way as power vehicles, first being formed in the fabrication shop and then being constructed in the main erecting shop. For the final CM&EE test, before the whole train is released into passenger service, the power cars are transferred from Crewe to Derby where they are married up with their trailer coaches. After a short period of train testing, if all is satisfactory, the new IC125 set is despatched to its operational depot.

After the present fleets of Classes 56, 58 and IC125 units are complete, the railway's locomotive new build erecting shops will be comparatively empty unless orders, for another design of diesel or electric locomotive, are placed or export contracts for the Class 58 design are won. Already on the advanced planning drawing board is a Class 88 long distance electric freight locomotive.

Plate 113: A locomotive for the 1980s. A brand new Class 56, No. 56098, painted in the 1980s 'Railfreight' livery, stands outside Doncaster Works paint shop after completion, but prior to being tested. When the revised colour scheme first appeared, on No. 56036, there was much criticism but now, after several years service, the livery has been widely accepted and is now applied to the Class 50 locomotives, as well as selected members of Class 47.

Colin Marsden

Plate 114 (left): After arrival of the sheet steel section from the British Steel Corporation and the various steel stockholders, the first time anything like a Class 56 locomotive can be recognized is in the fabrication shop. Here the pre-formed drag box, frame supports and side members are united for the first time. The locomotive under construction here is No. 56042.

British Railways

Plate 115 (below): With all initial framing, body panelling and support members in position, the frame of the first Doncaster-built Class 56, No. 56031, is lifted high in the fabrication shop in readiness for uniting with its trolley bogies and prior to its trip to E2 shop for general construction. In the foreground a pile of fabricated drag boxes can be seen. At this stage the body is painted in a green under primer.

British Railways

Plate 116 (right): As the rear cab bulkhead is part of the frame of the locomotive, this is installed at same construction stage, and the centre opening will be the engine compartment access door from the cab. On the buffer beam the draw hook position is already cut and the buffer positions are marked. The body of a Class 56 locomotive normally took approximately 8 weeks, from the day the frames were laid, in the fabrication shop, until being positioned in the new build shop.

Colin Marsden

Plate 117 (below): After fabrication had been completed, the frame was placed on trolley bogies and then taken to the paint shop for pre-build painting. This procedure ensures that no unnecessary corrosion occurs, and that, when completed, the locomotive has no parts uncoated. Mounted on former Class 24 bogies, with their traction motors removed, the frame for locomotive No. 56094 stands next to Class 37 No. 37044, on 19th January 1981, in the works paint shop.

J. Patel

Plate 118 (left): Once in the works E2 shop, general construction begins. Locomotive No. 56096 is seen here, on stands undergoing wiring, and one of the main cable looms can be seen to the left side of the cab. Much of the brake equipment has been fitted, on the buffer beams, and in the brake compartment, and is visible through the open bulkhead door.

J. Pate.

Plate 119 (below): One of the final stages of construction, was the fitting of the cab sections and wiring and piping the driving equipment into position. From the shell of the locomotive entering E2 shop until the locomotive took to the road for testing was normally some six months but time was flexible, due to other works commitments and the availability of components. No. 56094 nears completion on 22nd April 1981.

J. Pate.

Plate 120 (above): Depending on commitments in the various shops, the completed locomotive must spend a period 'on works' testing, which is normally carried out in the test house or in conjunction with a load bank vehicle parked in front of the main works buildings. After completion of testing the locomotive passes to the paint shop where, on 21st August 1981, No. 56097 is seen in the company of Class 55 'Deltic' No. 55002 *The King's Own Yorkshire Light Infantry* and Class 50 No. 50039 *Implacable.*

Colin Marsden

Plate 121 (below): No. 56089, minus its BR double-arrow logo, stands outside the paint shop after a final coat of paint and in the company of a Class 37 and another Class 56 locomotive. When painted, the blue is applied first followed by the yellow ends and white roof and, finally, the black windows and buffer beams. Contrary to public belief, the large numbers and logo are not transfers, but are hand-painted on to each locomotive.

Colin Marsden

Plate 122 (above): Having been painted and the 'on works' testing completed, the locomotive is ready for its main line trial. This usually takes place between Doncaster and Scunthorpe with a train of merry-go-round wagons. If any faults are found during this trial run, the locomotive is returned to works for rectification. Here, No. 56088 has returned to the building shop for minor engine repairs on 9th January 1981.

Colin Marsden

Plate 123 (left): Old and new together. A Class 08 shunter, No. 08044, slowly propels Class 56 No. 56088 back into the building shop after the Class 56 had suffered a failure during its test programme. Following immediate repairs the locomotive will again be tested, and haul a test train to ensure that all is well before allocation to its home depot.

Colin Marsden

Plate 124 (above): During the early 1980s only three of the BREL works have undertaken construction of new vehicles and, throughout much of the 1970s and early 1980s, the large works at Crewe has undertaken the construction of IC125 power cars. This view shows the works fabrication shop, with one of the prototype Class 41, later 252, cars under first stage fabrication. From here the shell will be mounted on trolley bogies and taken to the main erecting shop.

J. Patel

Plate 125 (right): The fibreglass cab section of the IC125 train sets are fabricated at BREL Derby Works and, after being painted in primer, are transported on converted 'conflat' 4 wheel container wagons to Crewe. Further work is then carried out prior to fitting. This photograph shows an overhead crane gently lowering the partly completed cab section on to a driving car.

British Railways

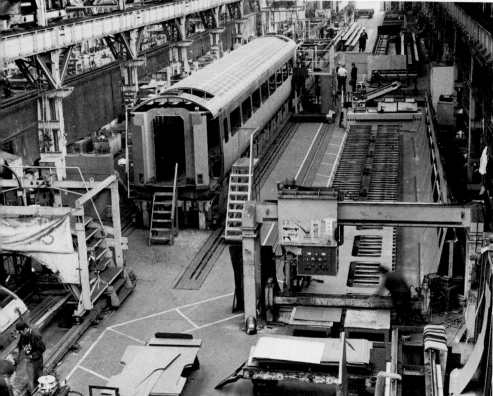

Plate 126 (above): A general view of the IC125 production line in Crewe Works. When the frames arrive from the fabrication shop, they are delivered to the far end and progressively move down the line as construction continues.

British Railways

Plate 127 (left): IC125 coach construction in Derby, Litchurch Lane, Works. In the centre of the picture, a partially completed coach stands mounted on workshop trestles and, to the right, a coach side can be observed in a jig. When a coach is assembled the two sides are fabricated together with roof and end sections. These are then affixed to a frame assembly.

British Railways

Plate 128 (above): The latest of the new builds is the Class 58 express freight locomotive. Assembly of these modular locomotives was given to Doncaster Works, who have had much previous experience whilst building the Class 56 locomotives. The frame of No. 58001 takes shape, on 21st August 1981, in the fabrication shop. *Colin Marsden*

Plate 130 (right): One of the design features of the Class 58 locomotive is that all major components are of modular design, and this means that such items as cabs, or engine cowlings, can be removed by undoing a few bolts, and are, therefore, easily replaced. No. 58001 has its cab section married up to its frame for the first time, during May 1982, in Doncaster Works E2 shop.

Plate 129 (below): With a partially completed Class 56 locomotive in the background, three Class 58 cab sections take shape, during early 1982, in Doncaster's E2 shop. With the modular construction method, the majority of components are fitted prior to the cab section being mounted on to the locomotive. The holes in the front panelling are for the fitting of headlight, marker lights, tail lights and multiple control jumper equipment. Above window height the two-tone warning horns can be seen. *J. Patel*

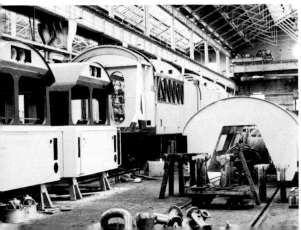

PUSH PULL SYSTEM

The push-pull method of train operation is not a new development, and was first used, back in 1905, with steam locomotive traction, on the LB&SCR with Class 'D' tanks. In recent years, to alleviate much light locomotive running and to facilitate quicker turn-rounds at terminus stations, various push-pull systems have been developed.

On the Southern Region, with the introduction, in 1962, of Class 73 (JA) locomotives fitted with high level air and 27 way jumper connections, it was possible to operate an electric multiple unit in multiple and control the locomotive, under the electric mode, from the remote cab of the unit and, thus, the basic modern push-pull system was born. From this the Southern Region system developed, and with the introduction of later electric multiple units and the final fleet of Class 73s (JB) in 1966/67, it became possible to start and stop the locomotive's diesel engine from the cab of the electric multiple unit.

The largest development to come from the locomotive/electric multiple unit push-pull combination was on the Waterloo—Bournemouth—Weymouth route where, on electrification as far as Bournemouth (Branksome for empty stock workings), a fleet of tractor units (4REP) was converted from hauled stock at York and fitted with 3,270hp traction equipment, and a fleet of TC (Trailer Control) units which, when coupled via the 27 wire high level jumpers to one of the tractor units, could control the tractor power from a remote cab. The complexity was such that a tractor unit could be sandwiched between two TC units and still provide the train's power.

The tractor—trailer—trailer system was operated between Waterloo and Bournemouth, but on the stretch forward to Weymouth, where no electric rail existed, a diesel tractor—trailer system was adopted. For this, a fleet of nineteen Class 33 locomotives was modified, with push-pull equipment, enabling them to be fully controlled, including engine start and stop, from the remote cab of a trailer or electric multiple unit train. The system soon proved to be very useful to the Southern Region and it was not long before the electric multiple unit trailer control/locomotive combination was seen operating on other than the Bournemouth—Weymouth line. In more recent years, they have seen regular operation on Waterloo—Salisbury and Portsmouth—Reading services.

Another operation on the Southern Region, which developed from the push-pull system, was the mixed formation train. Whereas in bygone days trains were usually formed only of vehicles with the same brake type, with sophisticated equipment being carried on the Class 73 electro-diesels, it was now possible to drive from an electric multiple unit train, have a Class 73 locomotive in the middle, and a vacuum-braked train behind. Thus the driver of the electric train would be working both air and vacuum brakes on one train, the air/vacuum being proportionally controlled via valves in the electro-diesel.

On the Scottish Region, when the Edinburgh—Glasgow line was being modernized in 1971, a new push-pull system, utilizing two Class 27 locomotives, one at each end of a rake of disc-braked Mk II coaches, was developed. This system proved satisfactory but, due to continued problems with the locomotives used, a further modernization of the line took place during 1979/80 and the Class 27 operated push-pull system was withdrawn. During the modernization of 1979/80, a fleet of ten Mk IIf BSO vehicles was adapted and fitted with a driving position in a section of the brake van, and were reclassified DBSO (Driving Brake Second Open). These vehicles were to form the remote driving cab of the new push-pull system powered by newly-converted Class 47/7 locomotives, with the push-pull control being transmitted via the train lighting and heating cables. Trains for this service, formed of Mk II or Mk III stock, have proved highly successful since their introduction and further systems, utilizing the same control principles, are likely to be adopted. A modernized Victoria—Gatwick service, which will be operated by Class 73 locomotives with rakes of Mk IId and Mk IIe stock and a converted electric multiple unit driving trailer will be introduced on the Southern Region from mid-1984.

Perhaps not often thought of as push-pull trains are HST, DMU, APT and the majority of electric multiple unit formations, as if a train is formed of one or more powered vehicles, it technically pushes in one direction and pulls in the other.

Another form of push-pull operation, still in use today, is for weedkiller trains, which have a locomotive at one end and a driving trailer vehicle at the other. Various engineer's, officers' specials and driver training operations are carried out with a locomotive propelling a saloon and are, therefore, push-pull, the relevant signals being relayed to the driver by a Motive Power Inspector, or guard, in the saloon.

The push-pull train system in this country has been a highly successful operation, and it is felt that further development in this field is likely in the future.

Plate 131 (above right): A push-pull train in the hauling mode. On the route from Waterloo to Bournemouth it is usual operation for trains to be formed with the traction (4REP) set at the London end, thus hauling the train of TC stock in the 'up' direction and propelling in the 'down'. Traction unit No. 3003, a 4REP (Class 430), hurtles towards Wallers Ash Tunnel, with a fast Weymouth—Bournemouth—Southampton—Waterloo train on 7th July 1981.

Colin Marsden

Plate 132 (below right): A 'down' country train, headed by 4TC (Class 491) units, with set No. 404 leading. All 136 cars of the TC fleet were converted from standard locomotive-hauled Mk I coaches, and the present driving cab was in one of the former toilet positions. The transmission of control, to the TC units from the REP traction units at the back, is via a 27 wire control jumper. Set No. 404 is passing Pirbright Junction, on 9th April 1981, with the 12.46 Waterloo—Bournemouth service.

Colin Marsden

Plate 133 (above): The Southern' fleet of 19 push-pull fitted Clas 33/1 locomotives was converted t operate in multiple with moder electric multiple unit stock and, i particular, the TC fleet. Thi system of operation is often use on the Waterloo—Salisbury route in addition to the Bournemouth-Weymouth line for which th operating system was designed Class 33/1 No. 33118 passe Wimbledon hauling two 4 T units on the 10.10 Waterloo-Salisbury train on 5th Ma 1981.

Colin Marsde

Plate 134 (left): With Class 33/ No. 33101 at the rear, a rake of T stock is propelled past Hampto Court Junction, with a mornin train from Salisbury to Waterlo during the spring of 1980 Although the locomotive is at th rear of the train the speed is in n way impaired, with a maximum permitted of 85 mph, (the maxi mum for the Class 33) compare to the normal 90 mph for the T unit, when in multiple with a RE unit.

Colin Marsde

Plate 135 (left): The most recent innovation in the push-pull system, a true advance for rail operations in the 1980s, is that operative between Edinburgh and Glasgow using Class 47/7 locomotives, pushing/pulling rakes of Mk II or III stock with a driving brake open second (DBSO) at the remote end. The Class 47/7 locomotives, converted for the service, are fitted with train lighting connections on their nose ends, together with a headlight. Here, No. 47701, *Saint Andrew*, races through Linlithgow, on 25th January 1980, with the 14.30 Glasgow–Edinburgh train.

Brian Morrison

Plate 136 (right): The DBSO vehicles were converted, by BREL Glasgow, from BSO cars and are now fitted with a small driving cab. The driver in the trailer car has a normal controller which, when operated, sends electronic signals to the Class 47/7 at the rear, via the train lighting cables. These signals are decoded on the locomotive which, in turn, takes the relevant power. Class 47/7 No. 47710, *Sir Walter Scott*, driven from a DBSO car, passes near to Linlithgow, on 29th January 1980, with the 11.30 Edinburgh–Glasgow service.

Brian Morrison

Plate 137 (below): Not thought of as a push-pull system, are the HSTs or IC125 train sets, but as the train has a remote-powered vehicle controlled by the driver at the opposite end of the train, technically, these are push-pull trains. Western Region allocated IC125 set No. 253025 passes Bathampton Junction, on 13th May 1980, with the 11.45 Paddington–Bristol train.

Colin Marsden

THE FREIGHTLINER SYSTEM

The 'Freightliner' system is based on the carriage of high capacity containers on high speed, specially-designed, rail wagons. These run in fixed formation (block) trains, made up of five vehicle sections, to provide fast and reliable services over medium and long distances at comparatively low cost. Like passenger services, these 'Freightliner' services run to a booked timetable. Most of the containers carried meet International Standards Organization (ISO) specifications, which aim to make possible the most efficient combination of rail, road and sea transport.

The original development of the 'Freightliner' concept was made by British Railways, and operations began, between London and Glasgow, in November 1965. Under the provisions of the 1968 Transport Act, the development and operation was vested in a new company, Freightliners Limited, which was placed under the control of the newly-formed National Freight Corporation (NFC). Under NFC management, 'Freightliner' grew to become the world's largest overland container haulier. After little more than ten years of very successful operation, the 1978 Transport Act transferred total ownership of Freightliners Limited back to the British Railways Board as a separately accountable company within the rail freight product portfolio.

Today, the 'Freightliner' network consists of twenty five terminals owned by the company and two owned by other bodies and eleven port terminals. A total of more than 200 trains operate each day and in 1981 the system transported 824,000 tonnes, providing a revenue in excess of £72.1 millions with a trading profit of £0.1 million.

The transfer of containers from road to rail, or sea, is carried out quickly and safely at purpose built terminals. The method of transfer is by means of specially-designed, and built, cranes, which can operate over the whole length of specially laid rail terminals.

Freightliners Limited has a fleet of over 7,000 containers of various types and sizes. They include covered, open and curtain-sided units. The company also carries containers belonging to other organizations such as shipping companies, which have large container fleets of their own, and containers of other private and nationally-owned companies like the GPO. The company also operate a fleet of over 550 road unit tractors, and 1,600 skeletal trailers of different lengths which are suitable for carrying the various types and size of container. The transportation system is flexible and a customer, himself, may deliver or collect a container, or this can be done by a 'Freightliner' vehicle. In practice, about 50 per cent of containers carried are handled by 'Freightliner' vehicles and the remaining 50 per cent by the customer's own vehicle, or by a haulier on his behalf.

FREIGHTLINER CONTAINER TYPES

External Length	Type	Special Features	Tare Tons	Tare Cwt	Cube Cu. Ft.	Payload Tons	Payload Cwt	Internal Length	Internal Width	Internal Height
Box 10 ft.	G	Roller shutter on one side	1	5	505	8	15	9 ft. 2½ in	7 ft. 7¼ in.	7 ft. 2½ in.
Box 20 ft.	L		2	2	1,085	17	17	19 ft. 4½ in.	7 ft. 7¼ in.	7 ft. 2½ in.
	L	8 ft. 6 in. high	2	3	1,162	21	5	19 ft. 3¾ in.	7 ft. 7¾ in.	7 ft. 10 in.
Box 30 ft.	X	Top and end door hatches	3	5	1,618	21	15	29 ft. 4¾ in.	7 ft. 8 in.	7 ft. 1¾ in.
Box 30 ft.	N		3	1	1,618	22	2	29 ft. 5½ in.	7 ft. 7¼ in.	7 ft. 2⅞ in.
	N	8 ft. 6 in. high	3	4	1,757	21	17	29 ft. 4¾ in.	7 ft. 7¾ in.	7 ft. 9¾ in.
Box 40 ft.	F	8 ft. 6 in. high	4	3	2,366	26	1	39 ft. 5¼ in.	7 ft. 7¾ in.	7 ft. 10 in.
Curtain Sided 30 ft.	BOALLOY	Load bearing curtains	2	16	1,643	20	0	29 ft. 5 in.	7 ft. 10 in.	7 ft. 1½ in.
Open 20 ft.	W		1	14	—	18	6	19 ft. 5¼ in.	8 ft. 2 in.	4 ft. 2 in.
Open 20 ft.	H		1	10	—	18	10	19 ft. 2½ in.	7 ft. 7¼ in.	3 ft. 0 in.
Open 20 ft.	T	Coil Carrier	2	14	—	23	5	18 ft. 9 in.	8 ft. 1 in.	3 ft. 0 in.
Open 30 ft.	Y		2	8	—	22	12	29 ft. 6 in.	8 ft. 2 in.	3 ft. 2 in.
Open 30 ft.	K		3	1	—	21	19	29 ft. 3¼ in.	7 ft. 7¼ in.	3 ft. 0 in.
Open 30 ft.	C	High point loading potential	2	17	—	25	3	29 ft. 6½ in.	8 ft. 1½ in.	3 ft. 1 in.

Note: Unless specially noted, all the above covered containers are 8 ft. 0 in. high and 8 ft. 0 in. wide externally
All have end doors

In addition to its activities within Great Britain, services to Ireland and the Continent are offered by 'Freightliner'. It serves all the container ports operating deep sea shipping services; indeed, with the growth of maritime containerization, this has become an increasingly important sector of the company's business. 'Freightliner' has also pioneered a container-based distribution concept, which eliminates intermediate warehousing.

The chief advantages of the 'Freightliner' system can be summarized as follows:

1) Speed: 'Freightliner' trains can run at 75 mph and travel up to 500 miles (London—Aberdeen) overnight.
2) Regularity and reliability: 'Freightliner' trains run on a strictly-timetabled daily basis. A reservation system ensures that space is available on the trains.
3) Size: 'Freightliner' is a nationwide business, and has the backing of nationwide resources.
4) Flexibility: 'Freightliner' can offer a complete door-to-door service, or undertake the trunk link in a total movement. It has different types and sizes of containers to match its customers' varied products.
5) Security and freedom from damage: 'Freightliner' trains travel fast to their destinations with no intermediate shunting.

Freightliner's competitiveness with other forms of freight transport has increased tremendously in recent years. Fuel cost increases, in particular, have improved the company's competitiveness, especially over longer distances. With the introduction of the new EEC regulations on truck drivers' hours and distances, 'Freightliner' comfortably outstrips the road haulier on journeys over 280 miles.

The basic facts:

25 terminals (plus service to 11 port terminals and 2 privately-owned terminals)
2,200 staff
6,000 containers
500 motive units
1,400 trailers
200 trains each day
£72.1 millions annual revenue in 1981
£0.1 million trading profit in 1981

This information is based on the 1981 figures.

Growth since 1974

	Volume 000s of tonnes	Revenue £m	Trading profit £m
1976	870	39.2	1.5
1977	870	46.1	1.4*
1978	843	51.0	1.7
1979	871	60.3	2.0
1980	866	69.0	1.4
1981†	824	72.1	0.1

For 1978 comparisons, this has been adjusted to £1.0m for change in depreciation policy
† 1981 figures affected by industrial action

Plate 138: Although the Class 47 locomotive is some 63 ft. 7 in. in length, it is dwarfed under the two mammoth 'Freightliner' cranes in the Southampton Maritime Terminal. Behind the Class 47 are some of the various sized containers available today, any of which can be picked up by the jaws of the crane, although some of the larger containers require an additional lifting frame.

Ron Cover

Plate 139: At some of the lesser used terminals, such as this one at Nottingham, much smaller cranes are in operation. The driving cockpit is conveniently slung so as to give good visibility when lifting the containers. In this view, a small open container is being lowered on to a private lorry.

Ian Gould

Plate 140: BR operate a sizeable fleet of 'Freightliner' flat wagons, normally semi-permanently coupled into 5 vehicle formations, with only the end vehicles being equipped with couplings and draw gear. All vehicles are fitted with air disc braking. Two trains of 'Freightliner' flats stand under the crane, at the Nottingham Terminal, during February 1982. In the foreground, to the right of the 'Freightliner' wagon, is the depot air braking test equipment, which enables brake tests to be carried out without a locomotive.

Ian Gould

Plate 141 (right): At Stratford, in East London, is one of the largest 'Freightliner' terminals in the country, and in this view one of their Stothert & Pitt Limited 'Goliath' cranes can be seen. These cranes are capable of spanning some four tracks, together with road-ways, and are able to lift 30 tons.

British Railways

Plate 142 (below): At some of the larger ports, where a railhead is not conveniently situated, containers may arrive at the port by road and then be loaded, by large container cranes, on to specially equipped ships. Here, at the Royal Seaforth Container Terminal, at Liverpool, three large cranes are loading container ships with the rail/road terminal on the right.

Colin Marsden

Plate 143 (left): A close up of the operating cockpit of a small 'Freightliner' lifting crane with the lifting sling, for various container types, hanging in the front. There are four retractable arms on the lifting tackle which are used for attachment to soft-sided containers.

Ian Goul

Plate 145 (right): Although the general trend in recent years has been a decline in freight traffic, one area of the country, East Anglia, has had an increase in 'Freightliner' services which is mainly due to the large docks at Harwich and Felixstowe, both of which are equipped with sizeable 'Freightliner' terminals. Headed by Class 47 No. 47017, on 3rd September 1981, an additional working, from Felixstowe to Harwich, is seen at Bentley Summit, near Ipswich.

Colin Marsden

Plate 144 (below): With deep snow curtailing all but essential train movements, Class 37 No. 37168 slowly passes through Doncaster, at the head of a heavy 'Freightliner' train from the north-east, whilst heading towards Sheffield. The container flat, directly behind the locomotive, is loaded with three small containers while the second flat carries two of a larger type.

Colin Marsden

Plate 146 (left): Many of the containers seen in traffic are not actually owned by Freightliners Limited, but by various outside companies which include world-wide freight hauliers. The Ford Motor Company, however, operate a 'Freightliner' fleet for the conveyance of components, and a train, formed almost entirely of their own containers, hauled by Class 37 No. 37288, passes Cardiff (Canton) and heads west.

David Nicholas

Plate 147 (below): In London, the two large 'Freightliner' terminals, at Stratford and Willesden, provide a considerable amount of traffic throughout the London sections of all four regions. Operating a transfer 'Freightliner' train, from Willesden to Millbrook, Class 47 No. 47105 passes along the Western Region main line, between Twyford and Reading, whilst hauling one 5 vehicle 'Freightliner' set and an air-braked 'car-tic' car carrying set.

Colin Marsden

Plate 149 (bottom right): A named Class 33 locomotive No. 33027 *Earl Mountbatten of Burma*, makes ready to depart from the Southampton Maritime Freightliner Terminal with a train, weighing some 744 tons, bound for East London and conveying fruit from South Africa. To the left of the picture three other trains are already formed for despatch to various parts of the country, and await their locomotives.

Ron Cover

Plate 148 (right): By virtue of their construction and air-braked operation, the 'Freightliner' fleet can operate at a maximum speed of 75mph, thus enabling them to operate on busy passenger routes without causing delays. However, as many of the goods transported are not available for collection until the close of business in many companies, the majority of this class of traffic operates during the night, in order to arrive at its destination in time for an early collection by the consignee. On 11th April 1981, Class 47 No. 47219 passes Fenny Compton with an 'up' 'Freightliner'.

Brian Morrison

MODERN COMMUTER SERVICE
ELECTRIC MULTIPLE UNIT TRAINS

Electrically-propelled commuter services in this country date back to 1909, when the London, Brighton & South Coast Railway (LB&SCR) obtained Parliamentary powers to electrify their main line and commuter routes by means of an overhead power pick-up system operating at 6,700 volts a.c.

However, this section is not designed to be a history of Britain's electric railways, but to deal with the modern electric multiple unit designs and types that have been introduced over recent years, with a large effect on improving local commuter services.

The Southern Region is by far the largest operator, in the country, of electric multiple unit trains, currently operating a fleet of 4,194 vehicles made up into 1,151 fixed two or four car units. Some 75 per cent of these sets are now over fifteen years old and only the fleets of Class 508 and 455 stock, introduced in 1979 and 1983 respectively, can really be described as purpose built commuter trains for the 1980s and can, therefore, be included herein.

The Class 508 four car sets were constructed, at York, to proven 1972 high density design, being a direct descendant of the prototype PEP stock used experimentally on the Southern Region during the early 1970s. As with all 1972 production type high density units, the 508s were fitted with 8 x 110hp traction motors, four at each end and two on each bogie, but these units are really 25 per cent underpowered as they were designed for three car formations for use on the London Midland Region. At the time of their completion the Southern Region was in dire need of newer electric multiple unit power, and an 'on loan' agreement came into force, with the units being delivered new to the Southern Region and being used there until their own purpose built Class 455s were completed. As the units that the 508 stock was replacing were mainly formed in four car sets, a fourth (TS) vehicle was added to the Class 508s to increase passenger loading, but this considerably reduced the units take-up speed.

The Class 508 units were fitted with many new systems, including single air pipe operation, dynamic/EP braking and an electronic wheel slide detection system, which had not been used before on the Southern Region. Following delivery from the York Works of BREL, at about the rate of four units per month, thorough testing, pre-service evaluation and crew training was carried out. At the commencement of passenger service with the new stock, one area that caused both public and staff concern was the air-operated sliding doors, which was yet another new system to the Southern Region. Many passengers would stand and wait for the doors to be opened, whilst others would try to force the system and cause damage to the equipment. After rather prolonged, but basic, teething troubles, the units have, by August 1983, settled down to an approximate 82 per cent reliability level.

Following numerous complaints by drivers the units were taken out of service, for some six weeks, in the autumn of 1981, the cause being severe wheel slip problems which were attributable to fallen leaves becoming compressed on wet rails. The problem affected the Class 508 units more than any other Southern Region stock, as the complicated anti-slip brake blow down system was operated if any wheel speed rose above the others on the

coach. This created a situation, in the most serious conditions, where the brake blow down was releasing the train brakes at such a rate that station and signal run-bys were not uncommon. Another reason why wet leaves caused unacceptable levels of wheel slip was that on stock fitted with disc brakes, the wheelface was never cleaned or scraped, whereas on conventional stock, friction brakes scrape and clean off any contamination when applied. Wheel slip problems were encountered on other regions operating 1972 design high density stock, but was not met by such hostile reaction as on the Southern Region. The problems were eventually overcome with the fitting of a wheel-slip over-ride button. If this button was pushed when wheel-slip occurred, and the driver's brake valve was in the emergency position, then brake control returned to the driver who disconnected the anti-slip system.

The replacement stock for Southern Region suburban services, classified as 455, was delivered to the region from the end of 1982 and commenced public service from May 1983. Units differ from the 1972 designed high density stock by having one motor coach, in the centre of the formation, dispensing with drum switch couplings/connections, and reverting to the time-honoured jumper system. During 1983, a total of 74 Class 455 units were in the course of construction and delivery from BREL's York Works. Following the introduction of these units to the Southern Region, the Class 508 units were reallocated to the Midland Region for Liverpool suburban services. Further fleets of Class 455 units were ordered during 1983 for Central and, eventually, South Eastern Division service.

On the Midland Region various fleets of commuter electric multiple units have been constructed to advance the railways towards the 1990s. The first fleet consisted of only four outer suburban/main line units built by BREL at York, in 1976 for use in the Midlands and classified as 312. These units closely resembled, in body design and technical specifications, the proven and well-liked Class 310 (AM10) units of 1966 vintage. The London Midland Region was also supplied with 1972 designed high density stock which was introduced during 1978. These were the three car formations, classified as 507, allocated to Hall Road (Liverpool) for use on the Merseyrail Northern line system. A total of 33 units was constructed and they are of almost identical design to the Southern Region Class 508s, the only obvious differences being their three car formation, non-passenger controlled doors and larger coach stepboards. The final London Midland stock to be included in this volume, the Class 317 units, were introduced during 1983 for the newly-electrified Bedford—Moorgate & St. Pancras line. After construction of these four coach units, at BREL in York and Derby, most of the fleet was stored at Bedford, or Cricklewood, until commencement of service in the summer of 1983, following the settlement of one man operation manning problems. These Class 317 units, apart from Class 210 diesel electric multiple units, are the first of a new generation of commuter train incorporating much design improvement from the 1972 high density stock. Construction of the Class 317 sets was divided between Derby and York, with the former works only producing the TC (Trailer Composite) vehicles.

The Eastern Region, with its electrification programme of suburban Great Northern lines saw, from 1976, the production sets derived from high density PEP stock used on the

Southern Region in the early 1970s. The Great Eastern three car suburban units, classified 313, were heavily modified, in external appearance as well as in the technical field, from the prototype. Class 313 sets operate on the King's Cross and Moorgate suburban routes. In addition, a substantial fleet of forty five Class 312 units, of the same design as those built for the London Midland Region, in 1976, was built between 1975 and 1978 for the Great Northern's new outer suburban electrified system and to augment existing outer suburban units, on the Great Eastern section out of Liverpool Street. All Class 312 units are of identical external appearance and the only major difference between London Midland Region and Eastern Region sets is that the former are restricted to 75 mph, while the latter have authority to run up to 90 mph. Great Northern units operate mainly on the King's Cross—Royston line, while those allocated to the Great Eastern section are used on the outer suburban Liverpool Street lines.

The latest addition to the Eastern Region electric multiple unit fleet are sixty one units which make up Class 315. Again, these are based on the 1972 designed high density stock and were the final derivative of the build. Units are four car sets taking power from the 25kV a.c. overhead.

These units were slightly different from their Class 313, 507 and 508 brothers as in the first forty sets, Brush Traction equipment was fitted in place of GEC, and thyristor controls were fitted to all sets. The 315s replaced the older sliding door Class 306 sets of 1949 vintage, and now operate over the suburban section of the Great Eastern, being allocated to Ilford.

The Scottish Region has only received one new set of electric multiple units for inclusion in this project. These again are a derivative of the 1972 high density stock and are classified 314. Construction was carried out by BREL at York, and a total of sixteen four car sets was built. Body design is the same as other 1972 high density stock and with power collection from the overhead live wire at 25kV via a pantograph. The sixteen units were introduced into service in 1979 and are used on the Glasgow suburban system. All units are fitted with thyristor control equipment.

From 1978 a total of 226 units of 1972 design have been introduced, operating on all electrified regions of BR, giving many thousands of passengers a more comfortable and reliable journey; all part of the continued improvement to nationwide passenger services.

Plate 150 (above): The design of electric multiple unit power for the 1980s, stems from the suburban prototypes of the early 1970s which underwent extensive trial running on the Southern Region. The units constructed were classified as PEP and, in this illustration, unit No. 4002, painted in experimental livery and undergoing trial running for the CM&EE section, approaches Wimbledon Park.

Colin Marsden

Plate 151 (right): The internal layout of the PEP units was new to the Southern Region. Apart from having sliding doors, which were designed to increase the passenger flow into and out of the coach, the actual seats were smaller in size, thus allowing more room for standing passengers. This feature the BRB carried forward into the production sets, but with revisions made to the seating layout.

British Rail

Plate 152 (above): A view showing two typical electric multiple unit trains, which were designed for passenger traffic of the 1980s. On the left, an outer suburban Class 312 unit, laid out for first and second class passengers, which was introduced during the mid-1970s to coincide with the electrification of the Great Northern section out of King's Cross. On the right is one of the true derivatives of the Southern PEP unit; a Class 313.

Brian Morrison

Plate 153 (below): The first production batch of electric multiple units, designed from the Southern Region prototype PEP units, was the dual voltage Class 313 units for the Eastern Region/Great Northern suburban electrification. These units, for all second class occupation, are equipped for a high acceleration and deceleration rate, an essential requirement for a modern transport system. An unusual feature of these units, when in normal operation, is that power is collected from the 25kV a.c. supply via a pantograph. However, when operating in the tunnel sections to Moorgate, power is collected from the third rail at 750V d.c. via bogie-mounted shoes. Unit No. 313028, is seen here approaching Finsbury Park.

Brian Morrison

Plate 154 (above): Once the modern electric multiple unit design was proven and accepted, various other areas of the country, requiring modern unit trains, were soon graced by their presence. The second area to receive PEP units was Scotland, where Class 314 units were to be found. These are three car formations, with power being collected by an overhead pantograph. Unit No. 314211 stands at Argyle Street Station in Glasgow.

C. P. Boocock

Plate 155 (below): Of identical appearance to the Eastern Region Class 313 and the Scottish Region Class 314 sets, are the Eastern Region (Great Eastern lines) allocated Class 315 four car inner suburban sets, which were introduced to replace the ageing Class 306 sliding door units of 1949. In this illustration, No. 315828 stands at Ilford, on 3rd August 1981, with a local service bound for Liverpool Street.

Graham Scott-Lowe

Plate 156 (above): On the Midland Region the only direct derivative stock introduced from the PEP prototype were the Class 507 units operated in the suburban areas of Liverpool. These sets were formed into three car units and equipped for third rail power collection. Branded with the 'Merseyrail' emblems, set No. 507021 arrives at Southport, on 17th September 1981, with the 10.16 Liverpool service.

Brian Morrison

Plate 157 (left): For the Southern Region, which was the last region to receive production high density stock, 43 four car units, of Class 508, were introduced from the end of 1979. All were allocated to Wimbledon and operated on the suburban lines of the South Western Division. Set No. 508003, with a commuter service bound for Chessington, passes West Barnes Lane, near Raynes Park.

Colin Marsden

Plate 158 (right): With the large electric multiple unit maintenance depot of Wimbledon Park in the background, an 8 car formation of Class 508 stock crosses over the pointwork, from the main line, to gain access to the depot. Following the introduction of Class 455 electric multiple units on the Southern Region, from early 1983, the Class 508 sets were progressively reallocated to the London Midland Region for use in the Liverpool Division, but with one trailer car remaining on the Southern Region for future use.

Colin Marsden

Plate 159 (right): The subsequent generation of electric multiple unit commuter trains, designed to improve passenger journeys for the 1980s, are the outer suburban sets which were first introduced, in 1983, on the London Midland Region St. Pancras—Bedford electrified lines and, later in the year, on the Southern Region in the form of Class 455 units. As can be observed from this production shot, of one of the first Class 317 units for the London Midland Region, inside York Works, a front end design change has taken place from the direct PEP derivatives, although the sliding doors have been retained.

British Railways

RESEARCH AND DEVELOPMENT

The British Rail Research & Development Section (R&D), whose home is at the Railway Technical Centre, Derby, carries out a wide range of studies in order to improve the services and facilities of railway systems. The centre, with its purpose built accommodation, not only undertakes work for its owning body — the BRB, but also for other British and foreign railway systems and networks.

The large centre at Derby, with 900 full time staff, was opened in 1964 to provide a facility where scientists, designers and highly-qualified engineering staff could work alongside each other in the quest for modern technology; a basic requirement for a modern and profitable transport system.

As well as the establishment at Derby, smaller area laboratories, for smaller research work, are located at Crewe, Doncaster, Glasgow, London and Swindon. To produce the continued high output by its staff, the R&D Section have to provide much intricate and sophisticated equipment for them to work with, as well as model and full-sized mock-ups of developments for evaluation and testing. This is provided by means of the railway's own test laboratories of which there are three at Derby:

a) The Vehicles Laboratory: This substantial building, covering some 16,200 sq. ft., was built in 1970, with the express purpose of advancing vehicle designs and testing various new and older vehicles. Many of the tests involve the use of the R&D's own fleet of specially built and adapted vehicles. The building is equipped with a roof-mounted crane and a sound proofed and air-conditioned control room where the majority of experiments are conducted, and where most data is monitored and collated.

b) Engineering Test Hall: This building, 170 ft. long by 192 ft. wide, houses the main workshops. The building contains many large structural and equipment test rigs, where bogies, frames and even railway sleepers can be placed under heavy prolonged and excessive loading. One part of the building contains a small vehicle workshop where modifications and the fitting out of the section's rolling stock takes place.

c) Track Laboratory: This smaller laboratory contains a small, but complete, section of standard gauge ballasted track where major ride/ground formulation and track behaviour experiments can be carried out.

Apart from these three major laboratories many smaller testing equipment stations, for signalling, revenue collection, computer engineering, etc., are housed in the various administrative buildings around the centre.

To carry out a full research service to the railway industry, the R&D Section operate two standard gauge test tracks where full 'on line' testing of locomotives and stock can be carried out. Test Track No. 1 is between Eggington Junction and Mickleover, a distance of 5¼ miles. This route has small shed facilities at Mickleover, where the equipment under test can be housed. Over the track length, various types of track base are laid, i.e., bullhead rail on timber sleepers, flat bottom rail on timber and concrete sleepers, continuous welded rail on concrete sleepers or fixed to the paved way (concrete bed). Sections of this test track are also fitted with hump/dip and lateral misalignment equipment to evaluate vehicle responses. Test Track No. 2 is between Melton Junction and Edwalton, a distance of 13 miles. This test track, often referred to as the 'Old Dalby' test track, also contains tracks based on various types of bed. The line has five tunnels in which various aerodynamic and acoustic tests are carried out. Sections of specially constructed (non-energized) catenary are also provided over a short two mile section for experimental work in the catenary, pantograph field. The maximum permitted line speed for the test track is 100 mph, which is currently reduced to 90 mph due to certain test equipments being in use. The Melton Junction—Edwalton line was primarily constructed for APT design and test work which used the, now withdrawn, gas turbine four car train.

One of the areas in which most enthusiasts hear of the R&D Section is by seeing one or more of the many vehicles belonging to this division. These, normally converted from redundant service vehicles, are usually painted in blue/red livery and carry an RDB prefixed departmental running number.

A list of locomotives/vehicles in use with the R&D Section, at the beginning of 1983, is given on the next page.

Based at Strawberry Hill, on the Southern Region, there are several test and experimental vehicles, which form part of the rolling stock development section stock; the work from this mini technical centre being mainly confined to electric multiple unit development. Much of the testing work carried out at this centre is caused from the refurbishing of Class 410/411/412 (BEP/CEP) units and Class 508/455 trial and development running. Most of the test trains originating from the depot are operated in conjunction with test car ADB970532 Mars formerly a Class 501 driving vehicle. Two other special test cars, Nos. ADB975808 and 975809 named Romeo and Juliet respectively, are currently based on the depot for chopper train control tests.

Plate 160 (right): An artist's general impression of the Railway Technical Centre at Derby. The main Research and Development buildings are marked; 1) Brunel House; 2) Main Engineering Test Hall; 3) Kelvin House; 4) Vehicles Laboratory; 5) Plastics Development Unit; 6) Lathkill House and 7) Derwent House.

British Railways

Locomotives

97801	(RDB968020)	(08267)	*Pluto*	Used for remote control tests
97021	(RDB968007)	(24061)	*Experiment*	Used for hauling test trains

DMU Vehicles

LAB 16	RDB975003 (SC79998)	*Gemini*	Battery power testing
LAB 16	RDB975004 (SC79999)	*Gemini*	Battery power testing
LAB 19	RDB975010 (E79900)	*Iris*	Radio signal testing
LAB 5	RDB975089 (M50396)	*Trim*	Track recording tests
LAB 5	RDB975090 (M56162)	*Trim*	Track recording tests
LAB 9	RDB975385 (M55997)	*Hydra*	Experimental railbus
R 1	RDB975874 LEV 1		Experimental railbus
	RDB999507 Wickham single car		Instrumentation testing

Coaching Stock

LAB 1	RDB975000 (M1003)		125 mph testing
LAB 3	RDB975002 (M1005)		125 mph testing
LAB 22	RDB975036 (W9234)		
LAB 11	RDB975046 (M34249)		
	RDB975076 Auto coach		Tribometer tests
LAB 17	RDB975081 (M35313)	*Hermes*	
LAB 12	RDB975136 (M34505)		
	RDB975146 (M15239)		Air conditioning testing
LAB 18	RDB975280 (S21263)	*Mercury*	
LAB 4	RDB975386 (S60750)	*Hastings*	APT coach tilt testing
LAB 13	RDB975421 (M34068)		Louvre test rig
LAB 6	RDB975422 (W34875)	*Prometheus*	125 mph testing
LAB 14	RDB975427 (M323E)	*Wren*	
LAB 10	RDB975428 (M9236)		
	RDB975429 (M15903)		Stores vehicle
LAB 23	RDB975547 (M81617)		125 mph testing
LAB 2	RDB975606 (S3068)		
POP	RDB975634 PC3		APT test coach. Purpose built
POP	RDB975635 PC4		APT test coach. Purpose built
LAB 8	RDB975636 ITV		APT test pilot coach
LAB 26	RDM395840 (LMS vehicle)		Ultrasonic probe coach
LAB 24	RDB901603 (B901603)		APT 'P' testing. Former trestrol wagon

Freight Stock

RDB999900 (Cov AB)	Tribometer test car
RDB951634	Brake van 20 ton

Apart from this fleet of special vehicles, various running stock items are occasionally removed from traffic for special testing purposes.

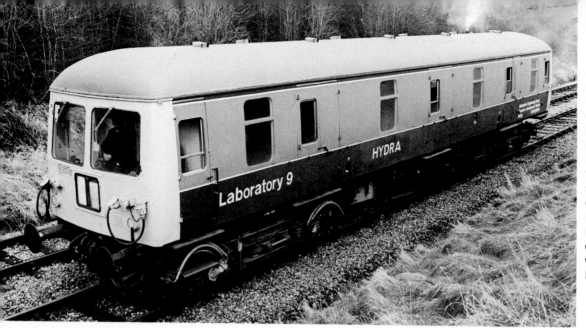

Plate 161 (left): Many withdrawn and life-expired items of rolling stock pass into the hands of the Research & Development section at Derby. Vehicles are often completely rebuilt, or at least receive different bogies, for their test programme. Cravens single car No. 55997 was taken over by the R&D section and is now numbered RDB975385 and named *Hydra*. It is used for experimental hydraulic control work and branded 'Laboratory No. 9'.

British Railways

Plate 162 (below): A Class 507 motor vehicle receives thorough testing in the laboratory. The control room can be seen at the rear of the coach, and a high pressure jack exerts side pressure to the front end of the car, just below draw gear height. It is usual for at least one vehicle of each new type constructed, to pass through the laboratory for testing, but not necessarily before taking up operations.

British Railways

Plate 163 (below): The test tracks operated by the Research & Development section are rarely photographed, but here is a general view of the track layout at the Mickleover end of the Eggington Junction test track. On the far right is a two road stabling shed where vehicles under test can be housed. When this picture was taken, test car *Hermes* and the Ultrasonic test train were present.

British Railways

Plate 164 (above): Laboratory No. 17, or test car *Hermes*, looks the same as a Southern Region multiple unit but, in fact, was rebuilt from a locomotive-hauled BSK No. 35313 and is equipped to operate with most types of train formation. This test car does not contain any traction equipment and, therefore, it always has to operate with a powered unit or locomotive, but it does carry a small generator to provide power for the 'on board' test equipment.

Colin Marsden

Plate 165 (right): Showing a mass of end equipment Research & Development section laboratory No. 10, car No. RDB975428, stands in the yard. This vehicle has a yellow warning end and a driver's position window, enabling it to be formed on to the front end of a test train. This vehicle was converted from M9236, a Mk I BSO.

Colin Marsden

Plate 167 (above): For the evaluation of the APT equipment, especially the tilt mechanism, a special test train was built, formed of three vehicles and often referred to as the POP train. The centre vehicle of the formation was of standard APT profile, while the two outer vehicles were only frame-formed. Test car pilot (laboratory No. 8) is pictured here. Note the experimental tilt bogies on which it is mounted.

Colin Marsden

Plate 166 (above): It is not only at Derby that research is undertaken to improve the railway system for the 1980s, but on the Southern Region, at Strawberry Hill, part of the electric multiple unit depot is now converted into a miniature Research Centre. Much of their test work involves electric multiple units and, to operate with their test trains a mobile test coach, No. 975032, was converted from a redundant Class 501 driving car. Until this vehicle was called to works for refurbishing, it was coupled, for mobility purposes, to a spare Class 411 driving car, No. S61035 from unit No. 7102. The pair are seen outside the buildings at Strawberry Hill.

Colin Marsden

Plate 168 (below): It is not only traction units that are developed by the Research & Development section, and one complete division deals with track maintenance equipment. One project under advanced design, during the early 1980s, was the Pneumatic Ballast Injection machine. This modern track maintenance machine was converted from a redundant ballast machine and, during 1983, orders have been placed for production vehicles.

British Railways

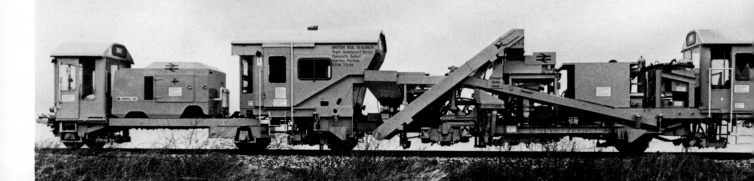